Dance of the Soul

Peter Deunov's
Pan-Eu-Rhythmy

Dance
of the Soul

Peter Deunov's
Pan-Eu-Rhythmy

Ardella Nathanael

Introduction by Don G. Campbell

Music and lyrics presented by
Vessela Nestorova and Barnaby Brown

Esoteric Publishing

Esoteric Publishing
P.O. Box 4092
Carlsbad, CA 92018

Cover design and illustration by Lightbourne Images, copyright 1997.

Printed in Canada

ISBN 1-889280-22-4

Dedication

This book is gratefully dedicated to the Master-Teacher Peter Deunov (Beinsa Douno) whose shining example, boundless loving, and Divine Wisdom has given Life, Joy, and true fulfillment to countless souls, including myself, and whose Light clears the way to oneness with the Divine.

Contents

Section I
The First Day of Spring

Section II
Enlivening our Energy Centers

Section III
Spiritualizing the Five Elements

Section IV
Working in Partnership

Section V
The Music and Lyrics

Introduction

From the very beginnings of spiritual expression, the gesture, the movement, the pace, and the sound of music have allowed people to move into transcendent places.

The power of movement, gesture, and music together creates a symphony that can orchestrate far more than any one component alone.

PanEuRhythmy now provides a simple yet profoundly moving way to orchestrate our daily praise, meditation, and thanksgiving. The simple movements, with their profound physiological and mental significance, bring consciousness to clarity, bring the body to balance, and bring the spirit to awareness.

In this wonderful book, Ardella Nathanael opens the doorway to Peter Deunov's brilliant work of music and movement. As you begin to experiment with these simple and yet profound exercises, you will find that the child within as well as the elder are joined together in the awareness of a spiritual, embodied presence.

This book holds dynamic keys for parents of young children, teaching them to move and express their bodies, just as much as for those who are in their elder years wanting to find simple and profound expressions that activate and maintain mind-body clarity.

PanEuRhythmy began in the first half of the century, yet its wisdom, simplicity, and profound rewards are easily available for the next millennium.

Don G. Campbell
Founder, Institute for Music, Health and Education

Acknowledgments

This book is truly a gift from the Divine Symphony of Life. Each of us in turn tuned in to the cosmic orchestra and found ourself playing our own unique part.

The first note was sounded on 12 August 1989, when I had a magical encounter at a PanEuRhythmy workshop in Phoenixville, Pennsylvania, with a wonderfully loving and spontaneous being, Sandy Taylor, creator of the "Rainbow Child Center." Sandy joyfully offered to follow me to another workshop and record it, which she did in Washington D.C. on 27 August, my late father's birthday.

The tune was picked up a month later, when, on my return to England, I was invited to teach PanEuRhythmy in Sheffield where I met an architect, Peter Paul Antonnelli, who urged me to write a book. When I told him it was already on tape, he arranged to have it typed for me at his own expense.

During the next few months, while I continued and completed my full time teaching job in London, and also conducted a PanEuRhythmy teacher training course, which he attended, the text was edited and mailed back and forth. Then finally, on 21 July, the day before I flew off for good to the United States, Peter Paul drove down to London with the completed book as a farewell gift, to launch me on my new life and venture of faith. I shall never forget the sense of awe and sacred trust which this generous, unconditionally loving and gentle act of faith in me inspired—on the eve of my departure in 1990 to a foreign country without work permit or financial backing, and with only a profound sense of Divine calling.

I am still in awe at the miraculous ways in which I was guided in the following year to Terry Pezzi and Hugh and Lesley Linton, whose open hearts, vision of greater possibilities, and untiring dedication finally made it possible for me to receive a green card to work in the U.S. To be registered here as a "resident alien" is amusing, but perhaps not totally inappropriate, as I generally consider myself a citizen of the universe.

After a long search for an artist in the United States who could capture the spirit of PanEuRhythmy, I finally tracked down by phone in her Scottish Highland home, that queen of PanEuRhythmy artists, Alma Dowle, who at once offered the gift of her magic touch

3

in expressing the essence of PanEuRhythmy in visual form.

The cosmic orchestra finally crescendoed in 1996, when, through the inspiration of Jane Seligson and the loving support, tireless dedication and visionary understanding of Brett Mitchell (to whom I am eternally grateful), this book—until then a workshop manual—was finally transformed into a work for publication. It was then graced by Don Campbell's heartwarming endorsement. My heart sings as I recall all these dear friends, including Barnaby Brown, who joyfully supplied the large color PanEuRhythmy photo, as well as the music and lyrics on which he had worked with single-minded devotion and inspiration with Vessela Nestorova, perhaps the closest person to the Master Peter Deunov still living today.

My deepest thanks and heartfelt appreciation to each one of you, and most of all to my many inspired and inspiring teachers of PanEuRhythmy. I feel a special love and gratitude to Philip Carr-Gomm, who first introduced me to PanEuRhythmy and took me to Bulgaria and connected me with so many wonderful people there. I am deeply indebted to Kroum Vagarov who courageously, wisely, and adroitly led the PanEuRhythmy camp in the mountains during the difficult Communist era, and personally trained me in the precision of the movements. My heartfelt love goes to Maria Mitovska, Kroum's faithful helper, who has lovingly mentored and unceasingly cared for me all through the years, and who has recently written her own beautiful book on PanEuRhythmy. My heart fills with gladness as I remember George Petkov, perhaps the most shining example I know of PanEuRhythmy and Peter Deunov's teachings, never ceasing to inspire us all through his Beauty-full, Joy-filled living and dancing. I am particularly indebted to Leon Moscona who opened my eyes with his remarkable insights into the inner meaning of PanEuRhythmy, and gave me a rigorous and unforgettable apprenticeship into the challenges and privilege of communicating it to others. I have also been greatly helped and inspired in my practice and teaching of PanEuRhythmy by the books (now out of print) by Yarmila Mentzlova and my friend, David Lorimer. I feel a special thankfulness and warmth for my friends, Alison and Barnaby Brown, whose enthusiasm, untiring work, and dedication to PanEuRhythmy and ever-fresh insights never cease to inspire me anew. To Viola Jordanoff Bowman, who has herself written two inspiring books on PanEuRhythmy and the

Master as she knew him in Bulgaria, I am particularly grateful for sustaining me over the years in this country (and through many lonely and difficult times) with her loyal friendship, warmth, prayers, and unwavering support.

I also want to say a huge thank-you to the many, many beautiful and wonderful people in the United States, England, Ireland, Brazil, Costa Rica, Australia, and New Zealand who have allowed me to introduce them to PanEuRhythmy, and opened their hearts and souls to expand my understanding of PanEuRhythmy and my own life's purpose. My heart fills with thankfulness as I remember you all and the countless ways in which you have each enriched my life and supported the work with PanEuRhythmy.

Above all, my heart overflows with joy and a deep sense of privilege and awe that my own life's pilgrimage attuned my being to the sublime music and heavenly inspiration of the work and teaching of the Master Peter Deunov, that incredibly loving, sensitive and celestially attuned conductor of the Divine Symphony of Life.

Ardella Nathanael
Christmas 1997

The Teaching and its Effect on my Life

Each dance of the PanEuRhythmy guides us gently and lovingly, opening us to the presence and power of Spirit that is within us and in the Universe.

It is impossible to describe this experience accurately, for it is beyond the realm of words, but I know the very first time I heard the music and the beautiful words that convey the meaning of each dance, that I was **home**.

The dances are beautifully simple, yet their depth and power is of a magnitude that cannot be measured. As I dance I feel deeply enveloped in the essence of Loving Spirit—I feel a union and communion with that spiritual essence that permeates all Nature and my being—a spiritual exchange.

The PanEuRhythmy weaves threads of pure love— PanEuRhythmy is LOVE IN MOTION—a moving meditation— opening me to receive and give, and healing whatever needs to be healed, restoring me to balance and harmony.

As I go about my day I retain that feeling. I feel more open and radiant—as if I am walking on a cushion of flowing love. I'm more open to my creativity, and when I play the piano I feel an awareness of a deeper dimension of my being, and a stronger connection to the music. The arm movements of the PanEuRhythmy seem to be transported into my piano technique, creating a natural fluidity and freedom.

I feel deeply nurtured by this beautiful dance. Its teaching is complete and total—embracing all life that is.

PanEuRhythmy—a teaching—a truth—a gift—an eternal guide weaving us through life—its meaning ever deepening, ever expanding, and from that still point within our hearts, we meet its gaze and quietly say, "Thank you."

Beverly Weil
1993

Foreword

I first encountered PanEuRhythmy in 1983, while running a meditation and personal growth group in London. I heard about a man who was a travel agent. As a travel agent, he was able to travel more easily in Eastern European countries which, at the time, were under the grip of Communist dictatorships and were not easy to explore. This man had discovered a dance which was a meditative dance movement which had been taught there before the Iron Curtain, but then had been squashed and suppressed ever since. As a travel agent he was able to go more freely than most people, and he formed deep connections with the people who danced this PanEuRhythmy.

I heard about him and invited him to our group. We were tremendously impressed by his whole quality. Our first experience of hearing about PanEuRhythmy from Philip Carr-Gomm was like opening a door into a new world we had always dreamed of and never yet tasted.

Philip began by telling us about how he had found out about PanEuRhythmy. It was a spiritual thriller story—an odyssey of danger, daring, trust, guidance, and joy. Philip had chanced on a secondhand book entitled "The Universal White Brotherhood" (which, in modern American idiom, might be transliterated as "The Universal Fellowship of Light" or "The Community of Light Workers in all Dimensions of Being"). His search for this community led him to France and Bulgaria—to the two places indicated in the book—with astonishing synchronicity.

Philip's then wife being French, they were about to vacation in France in the vicinity of the branch community led by Omraam Mikhael Aivanhov, a disciple of Peter Deunov, the adept who originated PanEuRhythmy. There he obtained contact names and addresses in Bulgaria. Then, on his return to England, the Travel Agency he worked for sent him as a tour-guide—to Bulgaria.

Americans may need reminding that, in the days of the Cold War and Kruschev's iron rule, travel to the Communist Eastern Block countries was fraught with difficulties and dangers. Contacting the local people could subject them to public suspicion, with possible interrogation, loss of livelihood, and even sometimes imprisonment, torture, and death.

Still, Philip risked showing one of the addresses he had been given in France to Marta, the Bulgarian woman escorting him back to the hotel in a taxi, and asking her for directions. To his alarm, her jaw dropped open and a long silence ensued. Finally she asked, "Who gave you this?"

He answered with studied casualness, "Oh, a man called Aivanhov."

Her face broke into a smile. "That's me!" she said, indicating the address.

Immediately he was connected with the mysterious inner circle of the followers of Peter Deunov, the Bulgarian teacher. This trip became the first of many, as he discovered his long-lost spiritual home and family.

Philip returned to our group to teach us the PanEuRhythmy he had learned in secret on those sacred mountains of Orpheus near the capital of Bulgaria, Sofia (meaning Divine Wisdom). We were entranced, and I could not rest until I had found a way of accompanying Philip on his next visit to Bulgaria.

This seemed to be the answer to what I had been looking for. I have always had a love of dance, though we had grown up in a family where dance was frowned upon—we were strict Protestants—but I found sitting meditation very difficult. I needed something which involved my body, my emotions—everything. This is what PanEuRhythmy does. All the differing strands of my life seemed to suddenly come together in that moment and weave into a bright new picture and vision of what life could be. It was also just plain fun to do, like any dance.

I had long been interested in Eastern European countries and how people survived under the challenge of spiritual oppression. How people survive in difficult circumstances has always intrigued me, and this is also what deeply impressed me when I did go over to Bulgaria.

I met people who had been dancing PanEuRhythmy all their lives. They were so strikingly different from the other people in the country who looked gray, oppressed, and heavy, who had just been squashed all their lives. These people had an inner joy, an inner life; they knew a secret. They brought new life and inspiration to us from the West! That struck me, how people who had so much less opportunity to learn, to grow, to expand, to enjoy life on every level, could be an inspiration to me. It was so exciting.

For the first time in a decade of visits, Philip decided to risk taking a group of friends to Bulgaria that summer under the guise of a regular group of tourists visiting the sights. We were to stay three days at a hotel at the foot of the mountains and travel up in the ski lift every day, to join the PanEuRhythmy camp in the highest mountains.

The inevitable official guide was allocated to us—even though Philip knew the country well and was perfectly capable of looking after us. But it was traditional in Communist block countries to always have a guide who would, as it were, keep tabs on us and make sure we didn't become too friendly with local people. Phillip briefed us and told us very strictly to avoid all mention in public of anything spiritual or pertaining to the PanEuRhythmy or Peter Deunov—taboo subjects under the repressive regime of the KGB.

It was important to conceal the real reason for our visit in order to protect the Bulgarians we were meeting with. Fraternizing with people from the West was not allowed, and PanEuRhythmy was considered dangerous by the regime because Karl Marx didn't teach it. Anything that Karl Marx didn't teach was suspect in Communist countries—yoga, the church, Tai Chi, anything. Everything had to be controlled by the government. We simply don't realize in the West the extent to which *everything* was controlled. Teachers had every lesson drawn up for them. They had to teach exactly according to the book. They would have Marxists listening in; the classrooms were bugged. They would be listening to check that the teachers were teaching exactly from the book and nothing different, to the letter. Bringing color, light, and life into that kind of environment was a miracle in itself.

Phillip went ahead of us to make certain arrangements for us. He arranged that the Bulgarian people who were dancing PanEuRhythmy would be waiting at the top of the ski lift on a particular time on a particular day when we would just come up there. You have to appreciate that he couldn't make any phone calls or write any letters because all phone calls and letters were carefully screened by the secret police. So he had to travel to the country, meet the people, and make the arrangements in person, then come back and fetch us! He couldn't do it in any other way!

Finally, our time came to be in the mountains. We drove as far as the road goes up the mountain, and then we were ushered to a ski hotel. It was rather noisy; there was loud dance music, and smoking and drinking at the bar, and so on. I felt a bit uncomfortable there, but I was looking forward, the following day, to going up the ski lift and meeting the people I had come to visit.

For me it was here that the supernatural intervened. At 5 o-clock, early on the first morning that we were due to go up the mountains, I suddenly jumped out of sleep and sat bolt upright in my bed. There was a loud voice which seemed to be reverberating throughout the hotel, which told me that I needed to be up on those mountains; it was my business to be up there, not in the hotel. I looked around, and my room-mate was fast asleep, so I saw that this voice had not wakened her. Very quickly I realized that the voice was within me; it wasn't an external voice. I knew there was nothing else to do but obey. I packed my ruck-sack while my mind sought very quickly all the implications and decided what I had to do.

This determination to be on the mountains posed obvious problems because of our guide. I didn't dare talk to Philip about it in the hotel as our conversation might have been bugged. I didn't talk to my room-mate about it either, in case our room was bugged. Instead, I wrote a little note which just said, "Can I stay up in the mountains tonight?" I put this note in my pocket to pass to Phillip under the table at breakfast—just in case the dining room was bugged, or even the table was bugged. I knew anything like that might be happening.

Phillip looked at me and raised his eyebrows. He didn't answer, and I knew why he didn't answer. He waited until we were outside the hotel on the way to the ski lift. Then he turned to me and he said, "You know, that's very dangerous."

"Yes," I replied, "but I need to do it."

He could see by the look in my eye that it was important, so he said, "Very well, then. I have already talked to the Bulgarian Communist guide, and told him that I'm very well acquainted with these mountains, and we're going to do some strenuous climbing! I let him understand that we could manage without him if he preferred to stay in the hotel. He's obviously a man who likes drinking and dancing. So it wasn't too hard to convince him.

"We'll ruffle up your bed and we'll make up excuses if he

inquires into why you're not around with the party when we come back."

I thanked him very warmly.

When we got to the top of the ski lift, the mountains were bathed in mist. The same Marta whom Phillip had first met very quickly took me and my ruck-sack to her tent, and put it away. The others went on to the place where they danced the PanEuRhythmy together. We then tried to follow them and lost our way because of the mist. So I virtually missed the PanEuRhythmy on that first day, though eventually we found the group.

This mist continued throughout the three days that we were up in the mountains. It was only afterwards—in fact it was the following year when I went back—that the Bulgarians told us that they had been praying for protection. For them it was a very risky thing to meet us, a group of foreigners, albeit up in the mountains. Anything could have happened to them; they could have lost their jobs, been put in prison, anything. They had been praying for protection, and, as happens so often, we don't like the answers we get or don't even recognize them as answers to our prayers. We had been looking forward to dancing in the sunshine and taking beautiful photos, but we were disappointed; it was foggy and cold throughout the three days in the mountains. The fog hid the views from us, and us from the vigilant binoculars of the Bulgarian police.

It was that evening up in the mountains when I was sitting by the fire, shivering in the cold mist, trying out the three languages I knew—English, French, and German—on the different Bulgarians there. One of them responded in French. I asked a question. There was a deep silence, and the answer came from a very profound level of being, out of that deep silence. I sat up, metaphorically and physically. I realized I was in the presence of someone of extraordinary consciousness. I asked the next question with greater care. There was a deeper reflection in consciousness, and I got an even deeper response. As this conversation grew and deepened, I knew that was why the voice had told me to come up in the mountains. I also knew that had this man opened his mouth and spoken to other people in his country the way he was speaking to me, he would immediately be imprisoned, tortured, and maybe even killed. I also knew that in England I had many friends who would be deeply interested and assisted by meeting him. So it was obvious; I knew I had to invite him to England.

It was a preposterous thing to do—impossible to realize under the laws of the time, when only the aged with relatives abroad to sponsor them were allowed out of the country. Yet, there are laws and powers transcending the human, and three years later Leon Moscona came to England.

As for me, I had no idea that my whole life would be set on a new course from this time on. When I got back home, it was only to find that my husband, a minister in the Church of England, had gone off with another woman, so that was the end of my marriage. I had given up my job to work with him in the Church, so it was the end of my career. It was also the end of my home, because the home was tied to the Church and my husband's job. So it was a complete breakup of everything. I had built my whole life around my husband, even though I was a career woman and didn't marry until I was into my thirties, but I did the traditional, feminine thing because I thought that was the right thing to do.

So when I got home, I forgot about the invitation I had made in the mountains because I discovered I no longer had a husband, a home, or a job. But the Universe doesn't forget, and the seed had been sown. Three years later, after a series of miracles, Leon came to England. He was given unlimited sabbatical leave from his job— unheard of in a Communist country! His Father died, so his responsibilities to family ceased. Somehow, the visa was produced. My friend Phillip produced the money for his air ticket because I was penniless at the time. However, I ended up looking after him, and a job manifested in time for me to be able to support both him and myself. For two years I fully supported him, both financially and by interpreting every conversation he had for the first six months until he began to be able to speak in English.

I traveled around with him. We went to Findhorn, Iona, and Glastonbury, all sacred places in England. We then went to Florence in Italy to a highly acclaimed international conference where he was invited to be the keynote speaker, with myself as his interpreter. I had a teaching job from which I could *not* be excused, and the conference was in the middle of term. Again a series of miracles occurred. I was told that the only way my employer could possibly give me time off—and it was unpaid leave—was if I could replace myself with a full-time teacher who would take all my classes, including my evening classes. Until two days before we left, we hadn't found anyone. Then, miracle of miracles, through a meeting at which the two of us were speaking, suddenly somebody came. She said she did it against her better judgment; she just knew she had to do it. She came to London, lived in my apartment, and taught all my classes—so I was liberated to go to this conference!

The miracles continued at the conference. We met wonderful people and danced PanEuRhythmy. Two severe financial tests occurred. I was mugged at noon in a well-to-do suburb of Florence while walking with Leon! The mugger was in a car, grabbed the handle of my bag, and drove off down the road with me still holding onto my purse (which had all my travelers' checks for us both), and dragged me with him. He was so furious that I wouldn't let go that he tried to break my hand-hold against the edge of the open car window. He missed and hit his own hand, and so was forced to let go. The remarkable thing was that I experienced no fear throughout, and even felt a sense of compassion for this frustrated, naughty-little-boy of a man!

The second test was the cost of the whole conference undertaking. Only months before I had been surviving on welfare. Now my salary was stretched to support the two of us. I had paid for two expensive air flight tickets to Italy, and we had been told the conference would be subsidized for us. We did not know we had been booked in the most expensive hotel in Florence and there were no funds to pay for that. The cost was going to put me in debt for the next three years. I prayed. On the last morning, with great trepidation, I went to ask for the bill; someone had already paid it and left the conference early! I am still moved to tears as I recall this gesture of incredible love, and marvel that I have still not learned to trust that my needs will always be met.

It was at this conference that we met Betty Rothenberger from California, who then sponsored Leon's visit to the U.S.A. That's how I came to be here as well, and PanEuRhythmy came to be introduced over here.

Leon's initial three month visa came to an end after two years; the British visa offices had synchronistically been on strike! As my apprenticeship in PanEuRhythmy also ended, I began receiving promptings, both outwardly and inwardly, that it was time for me to start teaching. Requests came from England and the U.S.A, and no one else could respond to them. Finally, I was invited by a community to come to the U.S.A. to teach for at least a sabbatical year.

The momentum was intensifying. How would I support myself? I was no longer young in years. How would I adapt alone in this new and vast country? If I gave up my home and job in England, what security would I have?

The first year was tough. The community didn't work out. My funds were running out. Friends were few and not to be stretched too far. I prayed for three signs confirming whether I was to stay.

The three signs were given, and I stayed. Like the widow's scant supplies, when she entertained Elijah, the funds have never run out. Friends everywhere have opened their hearts and homes to me, and unmistakable signs of Divine guidance and protection and even healing have come at unexpected moments, when most needed.

Through the amazing odyssey of adventures that make up my life, I am never allowed to become complacent—or bored! In my wildest dreams I would never have visualized all the adventures, excitement, encounters, opportunities, challenges, fears, personal growth, pain, and, above all, joy and fulfillment that have come my way through teaching PanEuRhythmy.

My heart is full as I remember all the opportunities to live my faith and learn and grow, and how even the most painful, threatening experiences turn to joy and expansion of consciousness, when embraced with thankfulness.

Introduction to Peter Deunov's PanEuRhythmy

I would like to briefly define what the word PanEuRhythmy means. **PAN** means "all-over," as in Pan-African, Pan-American, and so on—therefore nature, Universe, and the whole of creation; **EU** means good or harmony; and **RHYTHMY** means rhythm or movement. So **PAN-EU-RHYTHMY**, if you like, is the music and movement of the Universe. PanEuRhythmy is a dance-exercise-meditation intended to put us in tune with the rhythm and harmony of the universe. PanEuRhythmy opens us up to cope with the challenges of life at this time of expansion to global and universal consciousness. It was created to enable us to expand our consciousness and open up our understanding, our hearts, and our physical, mental, and spiritual levels of being so that we can attune to the increase in awareness, the speeding up of vibration, and the acceleration of events and evolution that are going on at the moment. As Isadora Duncan said, there is a great new upsurge of consciousness and quest for the ultimate dance of creation, just now. Mankind is at a crossroads. We could make a whole new evolutionary leap to a new level of consciousness, or we could extinguish life on this planet, altogether. It is so exciting to be teaching PanEuRhythmy at this time, because it was created precisely for this time, to help people all over the world.

PanEuRhythmy has qualities in common with yoga in that it's physical, and each movement acts on higher energy centers and opens up our consciousness. It works on the heart, through the music, and on the whole body and nervous system through the movement. It has qualities in common with Tai Chi, but it additionally has music. PanEuRhythmy is a meditation with deep inner meaning. I see each movement as being like a Japanese koan. Peter Dawkins, a leading spiritual teacher in England, said of the PanEuRhythmy (which he incorporates in his conferences) that it "enables people to attain deeper insights and understanding than they would otherwise obtain." The inner meaning of the movements is something that it would take a lifetime to deepen and understand. So the daily dancing of the PanEuRhythmy is always a beneficial exercise. In fact, that's how it's meant to be done, as a daily morning exercise at the start of the day.

PanEuRhythmy helps us to get out of the chatter of our minds, and to appreciate the true workings and functioning of the mind. One of the movements is called "Thinking." It's a movement which shows us how the true use of the mind is to be silently receptive to the higher, universal Mind, to capture those great thoughts which are just waiting for our consciousness to be ready to receive them, and then to work with them to evolve "Something Beautiful for God," to quote from Mother Teresa

Whenever one dances the PanEuRhythmy with others it is as if a link, a deep bond, is being created with those people. When one sees them again, it's like recognizing family—spiritual family. People who are from totally different backgrounds can dance together. Although they may not know one another to start with, by the end they just feel they belong together.

How is it done? I can only say that the music, movement, the concept has to be experienced. A very important part of PanEuRhythmy is dancing outdoors in nature. It can be danced indoors, but there is an element missing. It needs to be done preferably early in the morning, out of doors. Generally, when we dance, the sun comes out. Occasionally it doesn't, but I've known so many extraordinary times when the sun comes out, and we just seem to connect with nature. The animals and birds seem to join in. I've had clairvoyant people dance with me and say the little folk, the fairies, the elves, the tree devas, all join in. On one occasion someone told me the flower fairies left the flower bed and came and danced in the center of our circle. They were so happy to see human beings dancing a dance which approximated to their own.

Maybe that's the answer; because it's a dance that approximates to the angelic world, we are attuning ourselves to the true life, to the true essence of what is, to that which is most profound, highest, greatest, and universal. In doing so, all our faculties open. We discover universal oneness and our connectedness.

PanEuRhythmy was created by Peter Deunov, a great Teacher from Eastern Europe, to help us make this great evolutionary leap into the next millennium. PanEuRhythmy is a modern dance, but it is also very ancient, in that it is archetypal. The archetypes of PanEuRhythmy take us right back to the ancient sources of sacred dance, and they bring back the meanings and significance that have been lost in many other sacred dances. There is a universal revival of interest in sacred dancing. People are trying to get in touch with what originally inspired these dances, and through these dances find their connection with oneness.

The music is an integral part of the dance. It was also created by Peter Deunov, who was a great musician, an esoteric musician. He talked about different levels of music which work on different levels of our being: music that works on the physical level, such as jazz and rock-and-roll; music which opens the heart; and occult or esoteric music, which opens the soul and the spirit. PanEuRhythmy could be in that final category, spiritual music. It consists of twenty-eight dances, each with its own piece of music.

The music works on our higher energy centers. The music for each dance produces its own unique movement, and we dance naturally. This is borne out by the experience of many. A woman in Moscow who had learned the PanEuRhythmy wanted to share it with her pupils, who were only five years old. This woman was very brave. She knew that, as a teacher in the Soviet Union, it was totally impossible to teach anything other than the assigned lesson, which was prescribed for every day of the week by a central authority. Throughout the Soviet Union all teachers would be teaching exactly the same lesson to that particular age group. The classrooms would be bugged, so that the headmaster could listen in at any time and make sure that the teacher was keeping to the letter of the lesson. Of course, there was no freedom of access to books from the West; only Marxist-produced or approved books were available. It was like living in a straight jacket, mentally. However, this teacher discovered one lesson which gave her the opportunity she was looking for—a lesson of free movement to music. For some reason or other she was allowed to choose her music. So she learned the music of the PanEuRhythmy and played it as if she was just extemporizing—she was a very fine pianist—and said to the children, "Today I'm just going to play music, and I want you to dance around any way you like to this music." She played the PanEuRhythmy music and watched the children, and to her astonishment found that they were dancing the movements of the PanEuRhythmy. The music generates the movements in the same way that the sound of a tuning fork will generate a pattern in a sand tray or on water.

When Yarmila Mentzlova, a student of Isadora Duncan, first came to Peter Deunov, he asked her to dance to the PanEuRhythmy music and she danced the movements without ever having been taught. He turned to the people around to point out that the movements arise naturally out of the music for those who have ears to hear, and asked her to write a comprehensive book on PanEuRhythmy (which exists in French but is now out of print).

PanEuRhythmy brings great benefits to everyone who dances it. I remember a woman who was very overweight, very ungainly, dancing with great difficulty. Afterwards I learned that she had broken her Achilles tendon and had not been able to walk for three months. She was just beginning to walk again and was determined to learn the PanEuRhythmy. I went back to her area a month later, and she was walking like a queen, with such grace and elegance. Although she was still overweight, somehow she looked majestic instead of ungainly as she had on the previous occasion. Everyone in the workshop noticed, and when we commented she said, "I've been dancing PanEuRhythmy every day since your last workshop, in my garden early in the morning. It's made all the difference." She said, "Until now, I was used to just acting as if I didn't have a body; I was so ashamed of my body. Now I feel proud of my body. I feel good about my body. I feel a sense of grace just flowing through me." She continued, "My leg has now mended, and I'm walking equally easily with both legs."

I remember another man who was very stiff and rigid like a plank of wood when he danced. In the dance called **Jumping**, suddenly he was jumping like a three year old—we all jump like three-year-olds when we do this particular dance—and he just burst into giggles; he giggled and giggled and giggled! I was giggling and the whole group started giggling with him. His whole body seemed to relax. Finally he told us that he was from Nicaragua and his father had been killed in the fighting there. His mother was so frightened that she used to keep him beside her and give him work to do all the time because she needed help with the younger children. From the age of three when his father died, he had never been able to play. He suffered from lower back pain, and one could see it; his whole body was rigid. He said, "From now onwards I'm going to dance every day because it's loosened up my whole body. I feel like a three year old. I feel I've regained my lost childhood."

Personally, I used to have arthritis and it's helped me enormously. PanEuRhythmy loosens up one's limbs. Many people have found that it's helped with arthritis.

PanEuRhythmy has also opened up my mind and my consciousness. Every time I dance it, it's as if I were going up in a helicopter or a balloon from my everyday life, and I'm no longer seeing just that section of the road I'm traveling on. I'm seeing the bigger picture. I begin to see how different parts of my life tie in together. If I wake up feeling depressed or down, the depression lifts and there's a new joy that comes in.

Many other people have testified to this, and I can see this is the secret of that joy that I experienced in those people who were under communist oppression. It gives one that connection with meaning, with purpose, with the Whole which often eludes us in the humdrum course of our lives and we need to reconnect each morning if we're going to live our day fully and meaningfully. It's like switching on the light and no longer walking in the dark. Life is suddenly meaningful, colorful, bright, and alive.

Essentially we know that we are one with all life, and yet somehow our everyday experience is that we are fragmented. So we seek various practices to reconnect with ourselves—philosophy, movement, therapies, working through emotional releases, going to workshops, meeting friends, marriage, falling in love—all differing ways of discovering oneness. But this essential oneness is there all the time, and PanEuRhythmy is a beautiful way of rediscovering this.

PanEuRhythmy, being both ancient and modern, was given very consciously to help us penetrate to the inner significance and meaning and understanding of life and our Divine purpose. PanEuRhythmy helps us enter into and experience the symphony of creation—allegorically expressed in the ancient tradition of India in the dance of Shiva.

To quote from Peter Deunov himself:

> *PanEuRhythmy is the method which can help man restore his relationship with nature... employing air as the most modern, most effective, and fastest way of intercommunication... with the world and nature.*

Music is the language of the Spirit. The harmony of the spheres is a reality. The whole universe is singing; the sea, the earth, the whole starry system.

To develop a musical nature, you must focus your attention on spiritual values, for in the Spiritual dimension all energy and every living form finds its expression through the fundamental laws of music.

There is music in running water, in the blowing of wind, in the rustling of leaves, and in the singing of birds. When man develops his cosmic consciousness, he will become aware of the great symphony which can be heard throughout the universe. Only then will he understand the profound meaning of life.

As in all the spiritual traditions of the world, in the beginning of St. John's Gospel we read, "In the beginning was the Word, and the Word was with God and the Word was God." That is a very rough translation of the Greek, which actually means, "In the beginning God expressed himself, by uttering a musical sound, and that sound was creative. It was that sound that gave rise to all that is in the Universe." Now this may seem far-fetched, but scientists nowadays are discovering the truth of it. If you put a tuning-fork on a sand-tray or on water, every different note creates a different pattern. We also know that different music has different effects on us.

Stephen Halpern and other musicians, both East and West, have been researching the effects of different forms of music on the body, psyche, brain, and spirit—not only of human beings, but also of animals and plants. This research is now being used in a wide variety of ways, such as encouraging plants to grow faster and better, and cows to give more milk. One experiment on plants showed that, exposed to rock music, they wither and die, to classical music, they thrive, and to baroque music, they flourish and even wrap themselves around the boom-box!

John Diamond uses music to help people heal themselves. He finds that each different musician is working on particular problems within himself, using the music to express the way he is working through the problems and finding a resolution. People then are drawn to the type of music which is dealing with the particular problems that they are concerned with, and the music helps them resolve these problems.

George Lozanov, who created Accelerated Learning, was a student of Peter Deunov in Bulgaria. He discovered that certain kinds of music can greatly enhance learning—in particular, Baroque music such as that of Vivaldi and Monteverdi—and developed a successful method of teaching using music to accelerate the learning process.

Music, of course, appeals to the right-brain side of our nature—that side of our being which has been neglected so much here in the West, by our concentration on the left-brain training in our education. But the wonderful thing about this day and age is that we are discovering the importance of balancing these two.

Work is being done at the Monroe Institute and many other places on balancing the two hemispheres of the brain. PanEuRhythmy achieves this balance, so that we can then work, not as a split personality, but as a united, unified being, so that the currents of energy which rise through our being can connect at the highest point. As people are discovering from the ancient Egyptian symbols, the energy that rises up the two sides of our bodies needs to make a leap to connect at the top, and, when it does, people experience illumination and that higher mystical understanding which enables them to make sense of life. I think this is something we are all working towards. The exciting thing is that, as we approach this critical stage in the development of the human race, the great challenge is that we should make that leap of consciousness which will lead us to a higher dimension. In this way any imminent danger turns into a blessing, because mankind can then become greater, more whole than ever before, and the Golden Age which has been prophesied can actually come about; we can experience the Kingdom of Heaven on earth.

As human beings, we live upright like trees, making the connection between heaven and earth. Trees and human beings are both upright, and as such are conductors of energy. PanEuRhythmy very much helps us conduct that energy in a free-flowing way.

The music of the PanEuRhythmy is central and crucial to its powerful effect on every level of our being. It was created by Peter Deunov, himself a musician and composer of a very high order, and so transmits a Divine energy and connection with the angelic worlds and the world of nature. The movements alone do not produce and cannot account for the profoundly transformative effect of the PanEuRhythmy when done correctly, that is, with focussed attention and to the music of Peter Deunov consciously performed by musicians who love him and understand his teachings.

Each movement has its own unique music, or rather, each piece of music in the sequence of the PanEuRhythmy gives rise to its own unique expression in movement.

Some beginners seem to think they can bypass the music and just do the movements, but I have to point out that they will quickly become bored—as one tends to with movements practiced mechanically for the sake of physical exercise alone—and they will totally miss out on the profoundly exhilarating, inspiring, renewing, and healing benefits of the PanEuRhythmy as a whole. In fact, it is my experience that it is those people who go into it with real depth of attention, studying every detail, and practicing it with totally absorbed consciousness, who continue to practice year after year both alone and with others and who derive such profound benefits from it that they come to regard it with very deep reverence and awe.

Let me talk now more precisely about the PanEuRhythmy itself. The whole dance takes an hour and a half to perform. The first part takes three quarters of an hour, and is to do with the awakening of the human soul to its own potential.

Every single aspect of PanEuRhythmy is symbolic. Every movement is like a Japanese koan. It is something one can dance again and again, and each time penetrate more deeply into the understanding of its symbolism. I have derived my understanding of the symbolism of PanEuRhythmy from books by people who knew Peter Deunov, such as Yarmila Mentzlova and Viola Bowman, from working with Leon Moscona (a Bulgarian mystic and spiritual teacher who worked with me for two years in England), from my own understanding of PanEuRhythmy through dancing it and teaching it. I have also traveled to Bulgaria and learned from people who have been dancing PanEuRhythmy all their lives, some of whom knew and worked closely with Peter Deunov for many years.

I am not giving a final statement of what PanEuRhythmy is all about. This is simply my understanding, and I would like to share it with you, so as to kindle your own understanding. If what I say does not appeal to you, just dance the movements, as they are meaningful in themselves without any explanation, and gradually you will evolve your own understanding of what PanEuRhythmy is all about.

Strictly speaking, the whole of the PanEuRhythmy should be danced with a partner, but with small groups, for the purpose of learning it is often easier to dance the earlier dances singly.

The PanEuRhythmy is danced in a circle, counter-clockwise, with the music at the center—whether with live musicians or a cassette player. Having the music in the center of the PanEuRhythmy circle is crucial. The music expresses and represents the source of all creation, since all creation has its origin in the sound emanating from the Creator. "In the beginning was the Word" could be translated as "In the beginning was Voice/Sound/God expressing." Our dancing in a circle expresses our relationship to the center, the source, in a manner similar to the movement of the planets around the sun.

The counter-clockwise movement is also symbolic. The teaching is that, when the Divine spark incarnates on earth, the movement from Spirit into matter, the downward movement, is clockwise. (We are talking symbolically, of course, because it is not really downwards, but we have to use symbols.) The cycle of movement from the Divine into this material universe is a clockwise movement.

When we are thoroughly incarnate, when we are thoroughly in our bodies in this universe, the day comes when we wake up and begin to ask, "That's all very well, but what is it all about?" and other great questions. This is when we begin the cycle of evolution, of matter expanding into Spirit, with the cycle of evolution rising counter-clockwise. So PanEuRhythmy, which is the dance of spiritual evolution, is danced counter-clockwise around the circumference of the circle.

There are two other dances after the PanEuRhythmy, called **The Sunbeams** and **The Pentagram.** We dance **The Sunbeams** on the radii moving forwards towards the center and moving backwards out again, just like spokes on a wheel. This is the dance of those illumined souls who know why they are on earth, who are no longer on this earth for their own benefit, but simply to transmit the light and the healing and the goodness to other people. This is a path which I am sure we are all treading, to become Sunbeams to radiate that love and goodness from the Divine source out into the world which is sadly in need of it.

Once we have danced the PanEuRhythmy in a circle around the center and formed our connection with the center of all creation, we can then move on to dance **The Sunbeams**. Here we move in on the radii towards the center of the circle. As we dance inward we fill ourselves with Light and Love and then dance outward from the center to bring this gift of Light and Love out into the world.

The final dance is called **The Pentagram**. The Pentagram is a five-pointed figure, the symbol of man. You may remember the picture that Leonardo da Vinci drew, of a man standing in a circle, forming a five-pointed star. We start off with five pairs of people in a Sunbeam standing side by side out from the center facing counter-clockwise round the circle, and as the music proceeds, they all move forward eight steps. The two pairs of people who are the feet, move forward only eight steps and stop. The outer pairs of two (four people in all), who are the hands, move on another eight steps and stop. The two people who are the head continue on another eight steps (so that's 24 steps forward), and then stop. In this way they form a beautiful pentagram, a five-pointed star. As the music proceeds, they join up again, and then together they sweep around, like an arm of creation. After that they form another pentagram, and join up again, repeating these steps five times.

So you see the symbolism. We start on the periphery of life. When we wake up, we start to find our connection again with the Divine source, and to move on in the cycle of evolution, until we join those enlightened beings who can directly channel Love and Light from the Divine source out into creation. Finally, we take our place in the body of Cosmic Man—"man made in the image of God"—and manifest the Kingdom of God on Earth, the fullness of the Divine in every realm of creation.

PanEuRhythmy in the Rila Mountains of Bulgaria.

Peter Deunov at the PanEuRhythmy camp in Bulgaria.

Peter Deunov and musicians
at the center of the PanEuRhythmy circle.

Peter Deunov (Beinsa Douno)
Creator of PanEuRhythmy

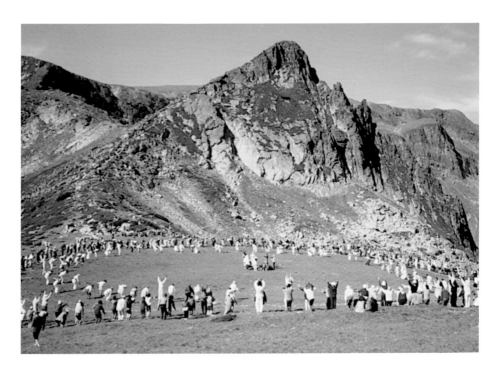

PanEuRhythmy in the Rila Mountains of Bulgaria, 1994

Ardella Nathanael
Teacher of PanEuRhythmy

Section I

The First Day of Spring

The first ten movements in Section One are called "The First Day of Spring." Spring symbolizes the awakening, not only of Living Nature, but also of the human Soul.

The symbolism goes further. The music is always in the center of the PanEuRhythmy circle, because music is creative. Peter Deunov always had an orchestra in the center of the circle. The music is in the center, because it is from the center of all creation that we are constantly empowered, that we are constantly created anew every moment.

I teach Tai Chi, so am aware of the movement of the spine. After going through the first ten movements I was conscious of how energizing the movements were. Doing the movements once again was incredible. I felt the energy push up the spine into the base of the skull. The process of movement had lifted the energy upward. Stepping toe first created spring-like steps that helped move the spine in a spring-like movement. These steps, coupled with the various hand and arm movements, reinforce the spring-like stretch of the spine and whole body. Each of the arm movements had a different effect and the cumulative effect was one of much cleansing and energizing. The arms reached upward to the side and downwards at various times. I am conscious that whenever the hands are moving, they activate particular areas of the body on all the subtle levels as well as the physical level. Certain movements help to open blockages. Others help to circulate the energy more fully. The hands clapping struck a chord and freed a stuck point.

It's hard to get oxygen and energy to the brain, and I sense that PanEuRhythmy does this increasingly as one practices. The stimulation of the higher centers occurs, as Ardella explained, by stepping toe first. The cycles of energy, perhaps spirals of energy, seem to increase the more one practices.

PanEuRhythmy seems a good aerobic practice for both the body and the soul.

Jane Edwards
Tai Chi Teacher

Movement 1

Awakening

The first ten movements depict the initial awakening of each person to what life is all about. We gently walk in rhythm with the beat of the music, starting with the right foot forward on the 1st, 3rd, and 5th beats, and the left foot forward on the even beats. This is important. The arm movements are done to the regular rhythm of the body walking, rather as the delicate melodies of violin, flute, and harp are performed against the backdrop of the bass rhythm of trombone, double-bass, bassoon, and percussion. In this way, the human body mirrors the orchestra, and I have noticed that people's dancing of the PanEuRhythmy closely reflects their own ease of handling the different aspects of life—physical, emotional, mental, and spiritual.

For instance, people who are very well grounded in their bodies will usually flow easily with the rhythm of the movements, particularly of the legs. Those who are highly sensitive to the spiritual dimensions will be delicately attuned to the subtleties of the arm and hand movements and will engage their whole consciousness as they dance.

As we move, we touch the ground with our toes first, before our heels. Peter Deunov suggested that we walk like this, because it has a very uplifting effect on our whole body, mind, and feeling nature. The modern way of walking, heels first, actually jars the spine, as many people have experienced. I have been experimenting walking like this, toes first, and it really has an incredible effect. One just feels as if one is a soul floating in this beautiful world, and that one has a vehicle, a beautiful body, but is not pulled down by it. This has a really liberating effect. One experiences being body, mind, and spirit all together, without being completely weighted down to the ground. The body then becomes alive, magnetized, and uplifted.

That is also the beautiful way in which the fairies move, lifting one knee with toes pointed and then the other knee. This is because they are light beings. In all these dances we can pick up some of their lightness and their joyful qualities.

The first movement, called **Awakening**, starts with the hands and fingers curled up on the shoulders. As we step forward with the right foot, our arms swing up and out sideways and our fingers uncurl and extend out horizontally. As the left leg swings forward, we again sweep the hands up and inwards, back to the shoulders, curling the fingers in again to the starting position. The arm movements are done in synchrony with the feet walking—the outward opening of the arms in a semicircle up and out to the horizontal sideways as the right foot steps forward, and the return of the arms up and back down to the starting point on the shoulders as the left foot steps forward. This outward motion of the arms to the movement of the right leg symbolizes the outward motion of the left brain connecting with the world around us, bit by bit, while the return of the arms, coinciding with the movement of the left leg, depicts the function of the right brain or feeling nature which swings us back to center and connects us with the whole.

An acorn which is buried under the ground, has within it all the strength and power, which, a hundred years later, will be a great oak tree. Each little seed has within it a power that is unfolding. Each of us has an inner potential, a Divine spark within us, which is all coiled up, but unfolding, like a little fern in spring. When the sun shines, the fern unfolds to the Divine light which is awakening its being and drawing out its inner potential.

The whole of life—the universe, everything—works in cycles. All the planets and stars move around the universe in cycles. We work in cycles of day and night, summer and winter, and birth, maturity, and death, and then going back into God, to manifest again in some way.

As we unfold to that Divine light, we also take it in, just as when we eat and expose ourselves to food, we take it in and assimilate it. When we expose ourselves to new ideas and influences, we need time to allow those ideas and influences to penetrate our being and to mean something to us. So the first movement, the opening and taking in, is **Awakening**, as it depicts the awakening of the human Soul.

Movement 2
Reconciling/Harmonizing

Once we begin to awaken, we discover that we are all at sixes and sevens with ourselves. We are out of harmony. So the second movement is called **Reconciling**, or **Harmonizing**, if you like. We need to harmonize the dualities within ourselves. In the world of Spirit we are all one, because reality is one, but here in this physical world, we live in a world of dualities—black and white, male and female, thinking and feeling—all the different dualities you can think of, as well as day and night, conscious and unconscious, and so on.

Before we can make progress we have to harmonize those dualities. We bring our hands together in front of the heart, because all harmonizing of unresolved problems takes place in the heart. We bring our hands together, symbolizing the bringing together of the polarities of the right and left brain, the thinking and feeling sides of our nature. Our fingers gently touch, and the healing energy flowing through our palms crosses the gap between them.

When we are learning to heal, we start by feeling the energy crossing the gap between the two palms. We bring the hands together, so that the energy can flow between them. Then, as our right foot goes forward, our arms swing out sidewards to shoulder level. The movement is very free and easy. Just allow the arms to swing out sideways from the shoulders, out and together again. You will find that the more you let yourself go, the more your shoulders will loosen up, your chest will begin to expand, your breathing will be freer and fuller, and—your heart will begin to open. You will take in more oxygen, more negative ions, more prana (as they call it in the East), and more healing energy. That is how the revitalization begins to take place.

Movement 3

Giving

The third movement shows what happens when we have established a degree of harmony within our being. We find our heart opens and we want to share. Our heart overflows and we just give, because we want to share the riches of life that we have been discovering. When we give, we find that the world gives back to us—other people, nature, God, whatever you like to call it. So the natural flow of giving and receiving begins to take place and becomes a very integral part of our lives.

The movement starts with the tips of the fingers lightly touching the spiritual heart center, located at the site of the thymus gland. To find the thymus gland, just follow the bony ridge which comes down from your throat into your chest. A little exercise you could do (separate from the PanEuRhythmy) is to tap lightly on the most pronounced bone of this ridge. You will find that this helps to wake you up and to make you more alert. This is because it is the seat of the thymus gland, and also the spiritual heart center or High Heart. (The physical heart is lower and slightly more to the left.)

As the right foot moves forward with the first beat of the music, the hands lift forward and up, while the arms and shoulders swing forward and stretch out horizontally with the palms up and pointing straight in front in a gesture of making a generous offering to someone. Then, as the left foot moves forward, the hands sweep back up and round and back down to touch the heart center again. This rhythmic, swinging movement of the arms accompanies the steady pace of the feet throughout, and produces a deep feeling of giving from the heart.

Movement 4
Ascending/Climbing

After we have opened to giving and it has really taken root in us, the joy of life really begins to bubble up within us. Life is too exciting and adventurous to stop at this point. We want to go further. So we develop discipline and begin to ascend the heights, because we want to make progress, to ascend.

When a mountaineer is climbing a steep ascent, his body, when he is really exerting himself, is inclined at an angle which is exactly half-way between the 45° angle and the vertical angle of 90°. That half-way point (between 45° and 90°) is 67·5°. When a mountaineer is climbing a steep mountain, his body will be at this angle.

Research has been done on the angles of the body and how they express in different levels of activity. It was discovered that this angle of 67·5° is exactly the angle at which the maximum energizing and awakening can take place in the human body. So in this movement, **Ascending**, we reach our arms up at an angle of 67·5°. At first it may seem slightly awkward as a movement, because we are moving the right arm and right leg simultaneously, but we soon get into it. Symbolically, this shows that we are reaching up first with our thinking nature, because our awakening generally starts when we discover some great idea. Our thinking nature is stimulated, and we reach up after more. Then our feeling nature, our heart, wants to follow. In this way our Ascending progresses alternately with the right and left side of our being.

As always, the arms move in rhythm with the feet. The right arm swings forward and the hand reaches up as the right foot steps forward, and simultaneously the left arm swings down and slightly back, the left hand stretching down to the earth, palm facing back. This movement of the upper and lower limbs of the same side of the body together induces a stretching of each side of the body alternately, stimulating each side of the brain in turn. (They could be likened to sideways stretches in

Hatha Yoga, except that, because they are done in a repetitive rhythm, we are hardly aware of the stretching effect.)

The effect of this dance is exhilarating, producing energy, vitality, and joy of body, mind, and soul.

Movement 5
Elevation/Soaring

After we performed the Ascending, a magnetic sort of momentum is formed within us, and we find that the two sides of our being are working in harmony. We want to do something with this, and this leads us naturally into the next movement of **Elevation**.

When the music changes, our left hand is up, and we keep it up on the next step, as we bring the right hand up to join it, so that the two are pointing up together at an angle of 67·5°. Then as our left foot comes forward again, our arms swing forward, down and back, again at 67·5°. This swinging of the arms forward and up as the right foot steps forward, then down and back as the left foot steps forward, continues until the music changes again.

This dance symbolizes the elevation of consciousness that takes place when people have been working on themselves for a long time, and this momentum really flows in their life. The two sides of their being, their thinking and feeling natures, are working together in harmony. They make incredible progress in developing themselves both as people and in elevating their spiritual awareness.

Movement 6

Opening/Expanding

The next dance is called **Opening**, which allows us to expand even further, this time horizontally. This movement/dance denotes that we are opening to the Universe all around us, outside the circle. With our mind, the thinking side of our nature, we are opening up to the great Universe, the Cosmos. We are enlarging our minds and opening ourselves up to great ideas, as we move round the circle. With each sweep of the arm out, we are opening to a different part of the horizon.

The opening out movement of the arms in this dance synchronizes with the forward movement of the right foot, symbolically expressing the function of our thinking nature moving out to connect with the world around us. As the left foot moves forward, the arm swings back to the heart, symbolically expressing the function of our feeling nature, which directs our attention inward to the heart and helps to develop our intuitive abilities.

To do this dance properly, the hand and arm need to be in a straight line, the elbow needs to be on a level with the shoulder, and the fingers must point to the spiritual heart center at the thymus

gland. Some people call it the High Heart because the physical heart is a little lower down. This is the heart from the spiritual point of view, and this is where we find the thymus gland, which controls all the other glands, and therefore truly is the heart of our being. The fingers are pointing to the High Heart, not covering it, and you will notice that this forces us to open our chest wide. It gives one a wonderful, expansive feeling, and as we swing the arm forward and out to the side horizontally we feel our consciousness going right out into outer space, into the Cosmos.

Halfway through the dance we change over. We put the right hand on the right hip, and we swing out horizontally and back to the heart with the left hand, so that now we are opening to the center of the circle—symbolically to the center of all creation. Our feeling nature is developing its intuitive capacities, and through our intuition we are beginning to get guidance from the source of all Creation.

I have found that when doors close in my life, (and many doors have closed, some of them very painfully), it is because I am being guided to something else which is greater and more important for me to do. If I just accept that, and work with it, the joy begins to flow again, and the meaning and purpose gradually become clearer within me.

We are opening up our heart in this dance. Again, the left hand comes pointing to the heart center, but not covering it. Then we open our left arm out to the center of the circle, where the music is coming from, and as we listen to that Divine Music, we are listening to the "distant drummer" who is setting the pace for our life. We are listening to our inner music, "the Song we came to sing."

Lawrence Le Shan cures people of cancer by helping them discover the song they came to sing, and John Diamond also talks of this. Each of us, deep in our inner being, knows that there is some great purpose for us in this wide world. When we can discover this Song, we can, as John Diamond said, *cantilate*, and life becomes an incredible joy and an amazing song. When we open up with the feeling side of our nature to this music which is inspiring and guiding us, our life can then truly become a song.

Movement 7
Liberation/Freeing Oneself

When we have discovered our inner Song, this great purpose, we find that there are things in our life which are stopping us from fulfilling this purpose. So we have to return to our lower nature, to our solar plexus, and to all those emotions and negative patterns which are locked in there. We have to break the bonds which are holding us back, to release ourselves from these negative programs which keep us from fulfilling our life purpose. Once we break free of these patterns, habits, and tensions, we can then sing the song we came to sing.

This is a very liberating dance, and it is called **Liberation** or **Freeing Oneself**. The movements in this dance have the effect of strengthening our willpower. Many people have reported that this is one of their favorite dances. After we have finished dancing this, there really is a sense of freedom.

We take hold (with both hands in a fist) of imaginary chains in front of our solar plexus, our power center. We break them and throw them aside, flinging open our hands as we swing our arms out sideways. Now, freed from our bonds, we step forward into freedom.

Movement 8
Clapping/Rejoicing/Giving Thanks

The next dance is **Clapping**, which is **Rejoicing, Giving Thanks**. The heart is now set free and we can fully be our real selves. The arms swing down from shoulder level and forward together, and we clap more or less in front of the heart as our arms swing on up and out, expressing gratitude as our hands open up to form a chalice. So gratitude makes way for Divine Grace to flow into our lives.

I am a linguist, and I like to look into the origins of words. I find that they teach me a great deal. The word "Grace" and the word "Gratitude" both come from the same Latin root. Gratitude is man's response to Divine grace, and Divine grace can only flow into a heart which is full of gratitude. If you really want to progress quickly, the way to do it—the key which I was given a few years ago—is to be grateful. Be grateful for everything that happens, even when you are going through great troubles, great trauma, great suffering. When somebody hurts you, thank that person; thank the Universe for the suffering. Welcome every event as an advent, because every event can become an advent if we respond with gratitude.

In this dance, as we rejoice we clap; we look up and our arms and hands open upwards. Our hearts and our being become like a human chalice open to receive Divine Grace.

This is the first half of the movement—the upward gesture. The downward gesture is equally interesting. As our hands drop down from the high point of the movement, they come close together in front of the heart, palms facing but not touching, before continuing on down and swinging on out sideways to form a horizontal line with the shoulders. This expresses the receptivity of the soul as it opens itself to become a channel for Divine Grace to enter the earth and radiate out into the world. Gratitude opens us to receive Grace, and Grace opens the chalice of our being to become a channel of Divine blessing in the world.

Peter Deunov demonstrating PanEuRhythmy.

Movement 9
Purifying/Sharing Subtle Energies/Scattering the Seed

When we get to the stage of **Purifying** we are really beginning to nourish others. From the experiences in our lives we have derived great wisdom, but this wisdom must be purified before it can really be of service. So we need to blow away the chaff and husks, so that others may benefit as we scatter these seeds of wisdom.

We begin this movement by putting the first three fingers of both hands in front of our lips and, as we blow on them, our arms gently move out horizontally to our sides, scattering them in the wind, without knowing how or where they will fall. In the same way, we can inspire others, quite unknown to ourselves. Often it is a throw-away word that someone says that just illumines something for us. Sometimes people say, "You know, when you said that, it really made sense. It just lit up my day and shed light on what I was doing," and one wasn't even aware of saying anything.

The important thing is that we work on purifying ourselves in both thought and speech, so that what we do and say is pure and, whether we are aware of it or not, it can bear fruit. So we purify ourselves; we purify those seeds of wisdom, and drop them on our way along life's journey.

In this movement, we give out energy from our center of higher creative expression. This is the energy which has been progressively rising through the last few movements, from the lower, denser part of our body, through the solar plexus and heart (in the movements of **Liberation** and **Clapping**), and which is now expressing itself through our throat center, as we make manifest the results of our inner work on ourselves. We also draw in to ourselves the subtle energies of

Nature to balance our own. This self-expression is the final stage in this first cycle of our spiritual journey. Our Soul becomes manifest, and we can finally transcend mere physical existence as, symbolically, we learn to fly.

Movement 10

Flying

The final dance of "The First Day of Spring" is **Flying**. When we have reached this stage we have, as it were, taken off. Having liberated ourselves from the difficulties and the grossness of our past, having awakened our finer nature and worked on ourselves consistently over a period of time (in all the ways symbolized by the first nine dances), we are now sensitive to subtler dimensions of being. Our discerning ability becomes keener, and we can truly begin to operate in the supra-sensory world. In other words, we begin to fly beyond the confines of physical reality. We are no longer earth-bound. We are in a body—yet not of the body. We are in the world and yet not of the world, as Christ said. We can begin now to move through life, no longer unconsciously at the mercy of everything, but consciously, as the pilot of our own vehicle for life and light and healing in the world.

The movements of **Flying** resemble those of a bird, and the main muscles to be used are those of the shoulders. This takes practice, but it is well to aim at a rippling, flowing motion travelling from the brain stem at the back of the neck, through the shoulders, the upper arms, gently through the elbows, and with subtle fluttering movements engaging the lower arms, wrists, fingers, and on out through the finger tips into the subtle emanations radiating out in the soft, ultra-visual colors seen by clairvoyants.

We have now transcended the physical; the soul is born, as it were, after its "ten lunar months" of gestation (symbolized by the ten movements of "The First Day of Spring"). We are now operating in the realm of the deva[1]—the life-force or energy-level of all creation—that which sustains the physical in living, manifest form

41

and gives it consciousness and life. We are ready to engage now in **Everá**, the true Dance of the Soul.

---

1. The Sanskrit word "Deva" means "Being of Light," and refers to all Light-Beings of the Divine world. It is the word from which "Divine" and "Divinity" are derived. (In Latin, *Deus, divina*; in French, *Dieu, divin*, etc. Our English word, "God," is from its Anglo-Saxon counterpart, *Gott*.)

Section II

Enlivening our Energy Centers

After the first ten movements of the "First Day of Spring," there are eighteen more movements to the PanEuRhythmy, all danced in a circle counterclockwise around the center, where the music is. These eighteen movements can be divided into three groups, with the first six being an awakening and spiritualizing of the energy centers within our being. Clairvoyant people often see colors associated with these dances—a different color for each. For me it has been a very great joy to teach the PanEuRhythmy and to hear the comments of different people. Very often different clairvoyant people have seen the same colors for the same dances, which confirms to me that this is so.

I've been doing PanEuRhythmy for about six years. I have done a lot of exercises over the years living in the San Francisco Bay area. The hour I spend dancing on Sundays is the one thing I do that leaves me feeling whole. I feel like my body, mind, and soul are all on an even keel.

At one time, I was the wife of a minister. Among the things I like about dancing around a tree in the park on Sunday mornings is that no one passes a collection plate, asks me to be on a committee or to wash the dishes, type a bulletin, teach a class, or devise methods of attaining the projected goal for the building fund. It is fun, healthy, spiritual, and it is free!

Suzann-Hagan
December 1996

Movement 11

Everá

Peter Deunov teaches that in the beginning there was one language throughout the universe, and he is not the only one who refers to this. All the great teachings of the world speak of one universal language. In the book of Genesis we have the story about the Tower of Babel, when the first language was splintered off into many different languages. We have the same kind of story in the Vedic (Wisdom) teachings of India and the Far East.

I love the books of C.S. Lewis, and in his science fiction series (*Out of the Silent Planet* and *Voyage to Venus*), he tells of a man who was taken to visit Mars and Venus, and how he discovered that there was one universal language. Until now the Earth has been silent as far as the universe is concerned, or whatever sounds we have produced have been more like a cacophony than a symphony. PanEuRhythmy is teaching us to blend in with the Symphony of Life, to blend in with the one universal language.

This particular dance is called **Everá**. It is a word taken from an ancient language which Peter Deunov calls *Vattaan*, which was very close to the original universal language. We do not know what it means, and, if we did, we could not express it in ordinary human language. For realities beyond, we do not have an adequate language. For example, people who experience leaving the body report that the reality they experience out of their body is such that you cannot express it in ordinary physical language. Our modern languages express physical reality fairly adequately, but are totally inadequate in expressing subtle and spiritual realities. So this word, **Everá**, is like a mantra; it expresses what it is. The sound expresses something which is beyond our left brain's ability to process.

The dance symbolizes the triad of Love, Wisdom and Truth. It speaks of how, once we have we have gained our wings and learned to fly, we have then an added dimension to our lives. We gain a great overview. We then have to learn to flow with the current, just like a bird, when it leaves the nest, has to learn first of all to use its wings and then to flow with the currents in the upper air. If it does so, then of course it does not have to flap its wings all the time. Once

45

it finds a current which is leading the way it wants to go, it can connect with the current. It may be a little difficult at first; you see it fluttering its wings, and then it just flows and glides on that current.

When it wants to go somewhere else it again has to flutter its wings, find a different current, and flow with that current. This dance, **Everá**, is teaching us how to do this, how to launch ourselves from a purely physical life, to go with the flow into a life of the Spirit.

To begin this dance, we face the center of the circle, with our hands palms down, then we swing to the left, connecting ourselves with the stream of Love. Love is something we experience through our heart, through our feeling nature. We then swing to the right and forward, our heart opening to universal Love which sustains and creates all that is. As we swing round on our right foot, bringing our left knee forward, our hands swing up toward our heart, palms facing; then, as we step onto our left foot, our hands reach forward and up. This gesture suggests a floating on the wings of Love—on and up towards Truth.

When we swing our arms forward and up, we turn outward from the circle. We turn towards our thinking faculty—symbolized by our right side— to connect with the stream of Wisdom. Love is the energy which can take us through life. Wisdom is the structure which directs us where to go. We need the energy of Love and the structure of Wisdom to steer us towards Truth. We have flowed with the stream of Love on the left towards Truth, forward and up, and now we swing out and back to the right, and connect through our thinking nature with the stream of Wisdom. Carried forward, then, on this stream of Wisdom, we swing around on the left foot, bringing our right knee forward, our two hands coming forward towards the heart, palms facing. Then we step onto our right foot, floating forward and up towards Truth.

Movement 12

Jumping

The second dance in the series is called **Jumping**. In this dance we start, facing the center, with our hands and eyes raised up towards heaven, palms forward, in a gesture of adoration and wonder. As the music starts, we bow down slowly to the ground, bending our knees. When our hands have nearly reached the ground, we swing our hands back to our sides and round to gather up the energies of Earth, then we raise them up to Heaven, as we jump up and clap our hands above our heads.

This dance is full of wonderful symbolism. As I said earlier, both men and trees have this function of connecting the material and the spiritual. This dance depicts something like what happens when lightning flashes. There is a flash of electricity, of power, of energy, that goes from heaven to earth, from the spiritual to the physical. This dance depicts something like this. As we bow down in awe and wonder, we bring down that great Divine vision to the level of ordinary everyday life. Then, as we swing our hands back, we gather up the ordinary everyday things of life, swing our hands up, and, as we jump and clap our hands above our heads, there is that wonderful gathering up of the earthly, of the common everyday, and raising it to its Divine potential. It is a wonderful dance for connecting Heaven and Earth.

Clap

Movement 13

Weaving

Now we move on to the dance of **Weaving**. Weaving the tapestry of life. **Weaving** is a gentle dance, very different from the jumping we have just experienced. Having established the vertical connection between heaven and earth in ourselves, we now move on to the horizontal, to weave the harmony of our interpersonal relationships. **Weaving** is the first dance in which we interact with others directly. As we move along on our inner journey, from working purely on ourselves to learning to interact with others, we go through a delicate process of becoming much more sensitive and adjusting to those who are close to us. It is part of the process of learning to "love our neighbors as ourself," for only when we can truly love the self in the other, can we weave the fabric of life, and that is what this dance **Weaving** is about.

In this dance we each take a partner. In a large group, the right-hand partner takes two steps forwards, so that, later in the dance, he can "weave" between his partner and the person immediately in front. In a small group, it is better to "weave" on the radius to and from the center, as you move sideways between the inner and outer circles. In this way we maintain our relationship with the center, which is crucial throughout the PanEuRhythmy.

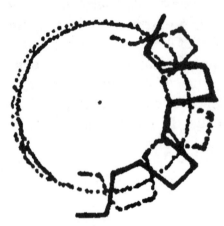

We start by holding our elbows out horizontally, our hands palms down with our fingers pointing towards the heart center, again at the level of the thymus gland. Then, as we bring our right foot forward, our arms swing out, pivoting at the elbows until they are straight out sideways horizontally from the shoulders, palms down. We then swing them back to the heart as our left foot steps forward. In this manner, we take eight steps forward, parallel with our partners.

Remember that we are walking around the circle, each on our own radius, very close to the radius of our neighbors, yet on our own individual impulse of creation. Each of us is a Divine spark; each of us is incorporating, or manifesting, one ray of creation. So in this dance it is important to be very attentive to your partner. When dancing around the circle, the person on the inside will have to take very small steps to enable those in the outer circle to keep up. This is also very symbolic of the way we have to adjust to our fellow travelers in our life's journey.

This dance occurs in intervals of eight steps—seven steps forward, and then the feet come together on the eighth. This is very significant because the number eight is the symbol of completion. There are eight colors in the spectrum (seven colors and then white, which is the blending together of all the seven colors of the rainbow), and eight notes in the musical scale (if you include the upper Doh, which completes the scale). Even the form of the figure eight is significant and symbolic as it expresses perpetual motion. The teaching is that a spiritual Master, when giving his energy to a disciple (if the Master is a truly great soul and not acting out of selfishness), will send his energy out to the disciple in a figure of eight, around himself and then around his disciple. This idea occurs in Elizabeth Haich's book, *Initiation.*  The master who is possessive and dominating with his disciple, will create a circle around himself and the disciple, so that there is bondage. But the person who is truly a great Master will give complete freedom to the person who is learning from him, and create a figure of eight.

In this dance you and your partner both take seven steps forward, and on the eighth step bring your feet together (symbolizing completion, the eighth "step" completing the cycle and so moving us on and up to a new cycle in the spiral). Then we cross over: the foot which is furthest away from our partners moves across towards them. The persons on the inside circle will cross over to the outside, and those on the outer circle to the inner—like the threads which cross over when you are weaving a piece of cloth on a loom.

We take eight sideways steps, crossing over between the partners nearest us, on a direct radius between ourself individually

and the center, and on the last step the feet come together. In this dance we are weaving together the polarities of our life, harmonizing the inner marriage. Marriage is not an attempt to become one, in the sense of becoming uniform or identical. Marriage is the complementary interplay of two opposites—a harmony establishing itself between two very different people.

Similarly, the inner marriage is the marriage of the two complementary opposites within ourselves: the conscious self and the unconscious, the shadow and the light, the male and the female, the thinking and the feeling, the right and the left brain. All these different aspects are not always easy to integrate within ourselves.

We have now taken the first steps towards going in toward the center, and working with a partner. It is true that when we work on ourselves with others, it is often easier to connect with the center of life, and access that divine purpose or connection.

Movement 14

Thinking

The next dance is one of those which Peter Deunov gave words to. In Bulgarian it is called MISSLI, PRAVO, MISSLI, which means: "Thinking, right thinking."

I like to think this dance is showing us the true workings and full use of our thinking faculties. It tells us the story of the way true inspiration comes into our minds, which can then be made manifest in the world. When inventors and great geniuses make their discoveries, what seems to happen is that, just in a flash, a great idea comes to them. Now this does not just come out of the blue. Usually it comes after a great deal of work. A scientist will often have to work and struggle and research for years and years before he makes a breakthrough. Madame Curie was such a person. She came all the way from Poland to France in very difficult circumstances and had to work extremely hard in order to do her research. She was tested and challenged in every area of her life, until she finally made her breakthrough and proved the existence of radium and its power of radiation.

In the case of Mozart, the inspiration started very early in his life. Mozart said he would get a flash of inspiration for a whole symphony. Then he would meditate on that inspiration, before beginning to elaborate on it and put it on paper. It would take him two weeks or more to be able to work out the whole symphony and write it all down. Finally it would take months to train the musicians to actually make that inspiration or symphony manifest.

A Divine thought can be transmitted in a flash to a person who is ready, but to actually make that thought manifest can take weeks, months, years, or sometimes a whole lifetime. That, of course, is our task as incarnate human beings in this world.

We dance this symbolic moment of breakthrough by stretching both our hands up to the right, above our heads, with palms facing towards each other. We reach up, waiting for the music to begin and for that inspiration to be handed to us from above. As we imagine and feel this inspiration being given to us, we take hold of it with gratitude and reverence and very great care and attention. We bring our hands down, on the right, keeping our elbows straight and our palms still facing towards each other. With our thinking faculty we are bringing that thought, that new inspiration down into the

material, everyday, physical world. Then we take it into our feeling nature. Our hands, arms still outstretched, swing across in front of the body just above the solar plexus and up to the left, and we connect it with every level of our feeling nature and with our intuition. We bring our hands down again on the left, and swing them back to the right and up again. We make sure our mind has fully comprehended all the meanings. Then, and only then, can we begin to work on manifesting our new inspiration or insight and elaborating it in the outside world—the feminine aspect of the creative process.

In the next part of this movement it can be helpful to imagine a ball in front of your heart, a great beautiful supple ball of life. That ball is, perhaps, planet Earth, a particular dream or project, our own

heart, or the circle of people we move among. That ball extends in front of us from the level of our throat down to the level of our navel. Pass your hands over it from the top around to the bottom, in a gentle caressing movement. We are putting out that new inspiration into the consciousness of mankind, into what Teilhard de Chardin calls the "Noosphere," the sphere of mind which surrounds our planet, Gaia.

With great love and gentleness and sensitivity, we encircle Gaia. We have to do it with gentleness and sensitivity, because new ideas often meet with great resistance, as we know from people like Galileo and others in the past who tried to communicate new ideas. This now becomes our life's work—putting that idea out into the world.

At a certain point the music changes and our arms move out sideways and horizontal with the shoulders, the palms of our hands facing out, and we gently stretch and press outwards three times with the palms of our hands. Sometimes this is called "upholding the pillars of thought." We reconnect with those pillars of thought which we have established between heaven and earth.

Another way of interpreting this gesture is that we are stretching out and enlarging our vision, which otherwise tends to narrow down as we become caught up in the complexities of everyday life. We take a moment to enlarge our vision, to keep our horizons expanded, to keep our sights universal and great.

Twice we interrupt the circling movement of our hands to make the three pressing-outwards movements. Then we finish by returning again, (until the music stops and our feet come together) to that circling movement, lovingly caressing Gaia, our Mother.

Peter Deunov demonstrating PanEuRhythmy.

Movement 15

Aoum

The next movement is a very beautiful one. It is called **Aoum**. This one is telling us the story of sound and its creative power. Sound is tremendously important. Sound is the creative energy through which creation happens. All the great traditions of the world teach that creation happens through sound. "In the beginning was the Word..." is a clumsily translated Greek expression which could be translated, "In the beginning, God or the Divine Principle expressed itself." In the beginning there was a sound or vibration. In the scriptures of India, the Sanskrit scriptures, there's a similar phrase, "In the beginning was Vac," which means "voice" or "sound" or "the word." In the beginning was Vac (*Vaach*); in the beginning was the Word.

We know, just from a scientific point of view, that creation happens through sound. If you sound a tuning fork and put it on a sand tray or in water, immediately there will be a pattern formed according to that sound. Each sound has its own pattern. We get it in children's books like C. S. Lewis's *Narnia* stories for children. Lewis talks about how the lion sang, and with each note that he sang, different flowers, different trees, and then animals came into being. So we have it there in allegorical form. This truth is very deep and is known to us both through allegorical and scientific means; creation happens through vibration, through sound, and through music.

Stephen Halpern did a lot of research into this. He tells us this planet vibrates at just under eight hertz, eight cycles per second. He has done experiments with plants, putting them in rooms with different types of music. The music under whose vibrations the plants flourished best is music which corresponds to that vibration and which is harmonious. Discordant music causes the plants after a while to wilt, grow sickly, and even die. So music has a very strong influence. Plants flourish under the right kind of music, and animals as well. As we know, cows will produce more milk and plants will grow faster with the right kinds of music.

Stephen Halpern also recorded people in different activities and states of mind. He found that the person whose vibrations corresponded most closely to the vibration of the planet was a very powerful healer in the act of healing. When I heard that, it immediately made sense. It was as if that healer, by putting himself or herself in tune with the planet was acting as a kind of musical instrument through which the music of the universe could be played and then transmitted to the person being healed. It reminds me of the idea that we are the flute through which Krishna plays his music.

Aoum is one of the most sacred dances in the PanEuRhythmy. It's a beautiful sound which is found internationally. In the Christian tradition we have it in the sound "Amen." In Egypt it is found in "Amun" or "Amin." In India it's the holy mantra "Om" which is called the mother of all mantras. Only the hermits in the caves in the mountains would use this mantra, because it's so holy it leads back into the unmanifest.

It's very interesting to look into this sound. It breaks up into three parts: Ah, Oo, and Mm—in fact, it actually breaks into four parts, because after the Mm there is silence. If one looks at this closely, it's fascinating. Ah is the sound that comes out of our mouths when we first open our mouths and allow our vocal chords to express themselves. So Ah is that first of all sounds. It's the first sound, Alpha, in the Greek alphabet; in fact, all the alphabets I know start with the sound Ah. If you say it, just easily and naturally, "Aah," it seems to express awe and wonder, a sense of "Ah! Wow! What a magical, wonderful universe we're in!" It's the excitement of waking up. It's also the energy of spring. In the Hindu tradition, the trinity is made up of Brahma, Vishnu, and Shiva. Brah-*ma* is the expression of that first sound, Ah, the energy of Spring, of the expansion of creativity in the manifest world.

The second sound is Oo. It's formed by our restricting the sound Ah by bringing our lips together. This is the sound of Vish-*nu*. Vishnu may be compared to Christ, for he is the manifestation of Love, or the Nurturing Principle. It's the ripening of fruit if you like. In springtime the plants are opening up, they're spreading their leaves and their energy in all directions. In summer, they concentrate their energy on the inner work, producing the flowers, the fruits, and the ripening to maturity. If you listen to that sound, Oo, there's that sense of fruit ripening in it, juice, oozing—that sense of Oo, indulging, enjoying, revelling in the fruit, in the beauty of the produce of nature.

Then we move on to the third sound, which is Mm, the sound of satisfaction. It's also the sound we produce when we close our lips at the end of the sound. Ah is the opening; Mm is the closing. We have that in the Omega of the Greek alphabet, the Alpha and the Omega, the first and the last sounds. So Mm is the satisfaction, if you like, of harvest, of a job well done, the end of the day, and the end of the year, the Thanksgiving holiday in the USA. Mm. It's the sound of satisfaction when we've finished eating; we've enjoyed what we have received. Then of course after the meal, we go into the silence, into the rest. The final sound is the silence—under the blanket of snow of Winter. We move into the silence, and in that silence, all the energies are brought back into the unmanifest, to renew themselves and become ready for the next cycle of regeneration. The final sound Mm is the sound of Shiva, who is the energy in the Hindu trinity of dissolving the manifest creation back into the unmanifest.

When a tree or anything else has performed its function, as when a fruit is ripe and has shed its seed, it starts decaying in the soil. There is a natural cycle of dissolving, or taking back into the unmanifest, that which has served its purpose. So the last sound is personified as Shiva, the dissolver—not the destroyer, as we say in the West, but that which takes back into the unmanifest all that has served its purpose, that it may prepare for even greater usefulness in the next Springtime of Creation.

We have to understand this dissolving. We've seen a lot of dissolving recently: the dissolving of the Iron Curtain, the dissolving of many forms and ideas which have served their purpose and are no longer useful in the world. Women particularly are experiencing this with the old ideas of marriage. Barbara Marx Hubbard talked about the new pattern of marriage being the woman who has the vision, the woman who inspires, and the man who is so inspired and caught up with this vision that he lends his strength to enable this vision to come into manifestation. More and more women are becoming the inspiration to their menfolk, and the men are full of admiration, and are ready to lend their energy and their strength to support a woman who can really inspire them.

Shiva is the mystic in us, the returning from physical manifestation back into spiritual unity with God. The word "mystic," starts with Mm, and that dissolving sound is the sound Mm.

These are the three basic sounds: Ah, Oo, Mm. In the West these sounds come out as "Amen." In the East the sounds are said together: Ah Oo Mmm, as "Aoum." It is the sound which embodies all sound.

The Sanskrit alphabet is based on these three sounds. From the opening of the mouth, the uttering of the first Ah, in the throat, the guttural consonants are formed: k and g. As we modify the sound Oo, other consonants are created. Then the final sound, Mm, gives rise to consonants like p and b, which we call the labial sounds, because they are formed with our lips. This dance, **Aoum**, is like a mantra, representing the sound of the universal language, which will put us in tune with the Divine. Many people use it as a prelude for meditation.

In this movement our arms swing alternately up forward and back at a 45° angle (different from the steeper angle of **Ascending**). It is a position which enables us to balance between the physical and the spiritual worlds, between the energies of Heaven and of Earth.

We start by moving our right leg and our right arm forward. We stand erect, not leaning forward, and keep our arms straight, our

elbows not bending. We rise up on the ball of our right foot, as we raise the right arm, and our left foot outstretched behind us momentarily leaves the ground. Then we lower ourselves as we lower our right arm and left leg, and begin swinging the left arm forward. Next we move the left foot forward, and, as we raise the left arm, we rise up on the ball of our left foot, and our right foot leaves the ground.

It is much more powerful and beautiful if we can sing as we move. We sing three times AOUM, AOUM, AOUM, then twice OHM, OHM, and finally AMEN, as in the Western tradition. This is the beauty of this dance—it blends together the East and the West; it blends together all the great wisdom-teachings of the world in one great symphony.

Movement 16

The Rising Sun

We move on now to the final dance of this section, **The Rising Sun**. In order to evolve we must work first of all on our lower energy centers, our lower chakras. Once we have laid the proper foundation, we can then work on the higher energy centers starting with the heart. When the heart is truly open and working in harmony, the inner sun of our Soul can rise.

We are told that this physical sun that we see is just a material counterpart of a much greater reality. That energy which has created the world, is like a Cosmic Spiritual Sun, which is quite beyond anything we can see or visualize or even imagine. It has a subtle counterpart, and the physical sun we see, is an even lesser counterpart. So there are, as it were, three levels of sun.

As we dance, we can visualize the physical sun at the center of our universe rising. Or we can take it to a deeper level and visualize that Cosmic Spiritual Sun rising within our being, rising within the consciousness of all creation, rising and taking its rightful place in the center of all things, becoming the conductor of the great Symphony of Life.

We start this dance with our fingers, as in **Weaving**, pointing towards each other at the heart center and with our elbows out sideways. We visualize the sun there before us, in all its glory, beginning to rise over the hilltops. It rises up, into the sky, and our arms rise up ever so slowly until they are directly over our head with fingers pointing up and towards each other, like the apex of a triangle.

Next, we bring the left foot forward, turn our palms out, and move our arms outward to a horizontal level. This depicts the sending out of the rays of the sun out into the furthest parts of the universe. Light overcomes darkness, and everything is raised to its Divine perfection.

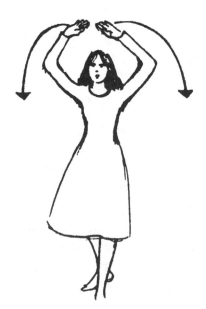

Then we turn our palms forward, and as the right foot goes forward, we sweep our arms around and forward and in to the heart. We slowly gather up all that wonder, all that joy, all that new life, vitality, inspiration and bring it gratefully, reverently, tenderly into our hearts. We repeat that movement once more, starting on the left foot.

Once our higher energy centers are truly functioning, our lower chakras are brought into play more fully, and we become fully realized beings. Our hands go down by the sides of our bodies and make six little upward-springing movements, palms facing up. These symbolize the fountains of living water, which joyfully bubble up in our being. This is a wonderfully uplifting, revitalizing dance. Four times we do these six gentle upward movements, raising the energy right through our being up to our heart—the fountains of living water gushing up and revitalizing us.

Then comes the final movement of this dance (very similar to Movement 3, **Giving**) when our hearts overflow. Our hands point to the heart, then move up and out forwards, and, as we take each step, we give and receive, we give out and we take in, finishing with our hands pointing to our hearts. To complete this movement, we pause for a moment, before repeating the whole sequence from the beginning.

There are a few things I would like to add about this dance. The words of the dance **The Rising Sun** were given by Peter Deunov, and the first words are IZGREVA SLANSETO which means "the Sun is Rising." This lovely word "Izgrev," which means "Sunrise," was the name that was given to the community Peter Deunov founded in Sofia. (The word, Sofia, or Sophia as it is written in the West, means "Wisdom," and I think that, too, is no accident!) The garden which was at the center of Peter Deunov's community still exists and is well worth visiting. It is like an oasis of peace and tranquility, deeply conducive to meditation.

Peter Deunov's body was buried in an oval flower bed in the center of this garden, marked only by the sign of the pentagram, with its five lines representing Love, Wisdom, Truth, Justice, and Goodness, which are the five esoteric steps in the Divine school of life.

The last words of this dance, **The Rising Sun**, are not in the Bulgarian language, but in the ancient language *Vattaan*. They are "Zoon Mézoon, Zoon Mézoon, Beenom To Méto." We do not know what they mean, but Peter Deunov said we could use them as a little song or mantra when we are feeling low. They have a revitalizing quality.

After the fountains of living water, the Kundalini energy, have risen in our being, and the two streams of energy have arced over at the crown, the heart overflows. Then we sing "Zoon Mézoon, Zoon Mézoon, Beenom To Méto."

This is like a mantra in the song. In contrast to Aoum (ah..oo..mm) which takes us to a transcendental state, almost a mystical connection, this mantra has an enlivening quality. These words open the heart and bring the bubbling fountains of living water up within us.

This whole dance can be sung in English to the following words:

Behold the rising sun, sending glorious light,
filling life with joy and pure delight.
Feel the living springing power flowing,
feel the living springing power flowing.
Zoon Mézoon, Zoon Mézoon, Beenom To Méto.

Section III

Spiritualizing the Five Elements

The third set of movements connects us with the five elements: Earth, Air, Water, Fire, and Ether, showing us how to tune in to their spiritual essences, and so raise the consciousness and potency of each to manifest more powerfully at a subtler level of being.

I have experienced the beauty of PanEuRhythmy as a cosmic, conscious dance. To discover its depth and meaning takes time and a realignment of oneself with the forces of nature. The physical energies come alive in the movement and in so doing help us toward transcending them and bridging the subtler cosmic energies. When physical movement, feelings, and thoughts are aligned one can experience a harmony that is ecstatic. The process for me has included dwelling on each of these three aspects separately before experiencing a flow in which there was a unity. These dances are truly a gift of love from our Master Peter Deunov, a love for humanity which will enable us to participate in our evolution as enlightened citizens of the universe.

Giselle E. Whitwell
December, 1996

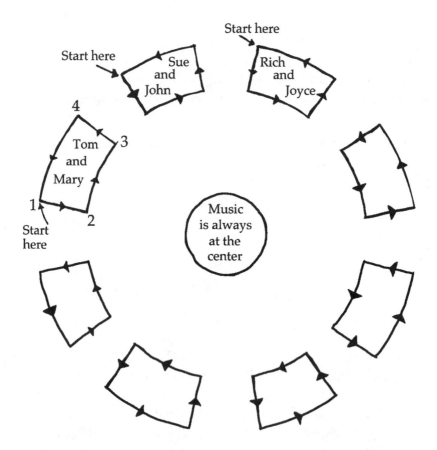

1. Couples stand one behind the other.
2. Couples stand side by side, right shoulders towards the center.
3. Couples stand one behind the other, backs to the center.
4. Couples stand side by side, left shoulders to the center.

The Square.

Movement 17

The Square

The first of these movements, **The Square**, represents the spiritualizing of the element of Earth. It is a very square, foursquare, earth-based dance. Standing in position 1, we face the center, our hands, as in **Weaving**, pointing towards the heart center.

We start by moving our right foot to the right, as we open our arms sideways and horizontally. Then, as we bring our feet together, our hands come back again towards each other. We repeat the movement, moving the left foot to the left and back, and then again, once with the right foot, and once with the left. Then we turn our palms to face forward, and move our arms up and out to the horizontal in a vertical arch, and back to the heart (palms still facing forward) as we take eight steps forward towards the center of the circle, turning to the left on the last two steps. Afterwards, we repeat the whole sequence with the right shoulder towards the center of the circle. (In this quarter-segment of **The Square**, we are moving clockwise—the only place where we move clockwise in the PanEuRhythmy.) We then turn left again, and this time we have our backs to the center of the circle, and so we move out to the outer

65

circle, to the outer circumference. Finally, we complete the square by turning left so that our left shoulder is towards the center and we are once more moving counterclockwise on the outer circle.

Now let us look at the symbolism. The way I see it is this: when we incarnate, we are born, as it were, on the outer circle and there we are—foursquare in matter, in physicality. But as children we are still "trailing clouds of glory... from God, who is our home" (as William Wordsworth wrote in *Ode on Intimations of Immortality*). We still have that consciousness of where we came from. We retain that intuitive awareness.

In the ancient Vedic (Wisdom) tradition of India, they talk of human life having four stages: childhood, discipleship, adulthood and Vána-prastha (the forest stage, when we give up all worldly commitments, possessions and move into the forests as hermits to prepare for transiting out of this life and into the next).

At the beginning of **The Square** we are facing the center, and for the early years of our life we are facing the Light. We are joyfully going towards the center of the circle, the Source of all life. When we are not fully aware of the Source, we have our parents to represent it for us, so all is well and we joyfully make our way towards the center.

We then turn left and start moving in the inner circle. This represents the stage when we need teachers (other than our parents). In the Eastern Indian tradition, children are, until puberty, in the care of the guru (Gu=darkness and Ru=light, so a guru is one who can lead you from darkness into the light). The true spiritual Teacher can initiate us into the Inner Circle, where, close to the center and Source of all life, we can learn how to apply this knowledge to our human existence; we are moving in a clockwise direction, so we are getting more and more involved in matter, in this world, in the ordinary things of everyday life.

Then there comes a point when our education is finished and we have to turn our backs on the Source and go right out into the world. This is like the teenager to adult stage, when we have to leave all that has been helping us until now—our parents, our background, even our spiritual tradition. I believe this is why young people rebel against their parents, turn to drugs, and try everything—because they have to make that journey on their own, away from the light at the center, away from the Divine music, the center Source, the home, out into the outer darkness. If, in their preparation with their Teacher, they have successfully internalized the Light, now they can move out into the darkness confidently, spreading the Light wherever they go.

The final stage is again counterclockwise, around the outer circumference of the circle. We evolve out of this life by completing all that we came here to do and by attuning to eternity and Spirit in preparation for moving on to the next stage of Life.

Now there is another dimension also. We are told that we go through all the signs of the zodiac, but it is not until we have gone through all of them that we wake up and begin to ask ourselves, "What is the purpose of life; what am I doing here?" We then have to go round them again, this time in the other direction—counterclockwise. This second time around, if we are awake and conscious, then we are truly on a path towards becoming Masters. We have the opportunity to move on towards the higher echelons of the human race. We are no longer just victims or ordinary human beings, living in a partial way, not fully manifesting all that we are capable of being, but instead are fully in charge of our own lives and in tune with the greater World Vision (as described in *The Celestine Prophecy* and *The Tenth Insight*.)

In the dance, **The Square**, we go round twice. We come back to where we started, and again we move towards the center. Perhaps our cockiness has now been knocked out of us, but in any case, if we are going to complete this task of incarnation satisfactorily, we are going to have to wake up and take note.

I see this as a picture of what happens in life. We have to go twice round the zodiac, so we go twice round the square. If we have awakened after the first time round, we can really achieve mastery of life and Self-realization this second time around.

When we move around the second time on the inner circle, even though we are going on the path of involution, we are hopefully doing it with greater consciousness. We really take in all the Light, Direction, Love and Wisdom that comes from the center, so when we have to turn our backs on the Light, this time we can really confidently take the Light out into the world. We can face the darkness because we have internalized that Light, that Vision from the center. Then we can complete the circle, complete our work and we are ready to move on to more subtle levels of being and work.

I believe that what I have said about going around twice is very much our challenge. When we are incarnated in solid matter, we have to go through it more than once, and hopefully on the second time round we get it right. If we do get it right, then we can raise the consciousness of earth, and the earth can become a paradise. Our human bodies can become subtle bodies, just as Elijah managed to transfigure his body. Jesus and Enoch also had physical bodies that they lived in perfectly and so did not have to pass through death. They were literally able to transform and transfigure their bodies and raise them to a higher level of being. The teaching is that the great masters of the world can materialize and dematerialize their bodies at will, because they have completed that task of spiritualizing Earth.

Movement 18

Beauty

The next task is to spiritualize the element of Air, and the dance for this is **Beauty**. Now the element of Air is the element of mind. Subtle Air is the mental atmosphere, the noosphere. We need space, and we literally need air to think. Our minds will not work if we do not get enough oxygen to breathe. The element of Air is very important. The mind functions in Air and when we think, our eyes go out and up, as our consciousness moves out into space.

We spiritualize the element of Air by beautifying the thoughts in our minds. As human beings we are all working on this challenge of beautifying our minds, so that they can express the Divine realm of being—purifying our thoughts, filling our minds with positive thoughts, using affirmations, praying, connecting with the Divine, and so beautifying the subtle element of Air. Of course in this day and age we are faced with another challenge—to beautify and purify the gross element of Air as well, because at the moment we are polluting it so badly, that there is danger to all life on this planet.

In **Beauty**, we start with our right hand up. There are levels upon levels of meaning for this. **Beauty** is like the bird floating on the Air. We float and sway on the Air forward and backwards. Then we sweep our arm down, past our body and back, while bringing the other arm up and the other leg forward, swing round, and sway again forwards and backwards. As with **Aoum**, we move the leg and arm of the same side together. We feel the element of Air under our arms, as a bird floating through the currents of Air. Feel that beauty of the bird floating on the element of Air.

Beauty, along with Truth and Goodness, is one of the three essentials for life and growth. We nourish our souls on beauty, as we nourish our bodies with food. If we fill our minds with beauty, we contribute to the well-being of ourselves and all around us. Ugliness depresses and saps our energy. Beauty enlivens, uplifts and gives new life, hope, energy and vision, for "Without Vision, the people perish."

Movement 19
Flowing

The next movement is **Flowing**, and it seems to work with the subtle element of Water. Water connects everything on the planet. Water connects all cells in a body together. Without water our cells would disintegrate and our bodies would not function. Similarly, water flows between all segments of earth and connects all together.

In C.S. Lewis' book, *Voyage to Venus*, the whole population of the planet lives on water. There is no solid ground. It is when they have what they call "fixed land" that things start to go downhill, and evil appears. As long as they live on the Water element, on the floating islands, they have that connection with the flow, the love, the creative element and Divine plan.

Flowing is a very important part of our lives. As soon as we become rigid and stuck on the gross element of Earth, we become calcified, and so completely caught up in matter that we fail to fulfill our Divine purpose. Mankind has to remain mobile and flexible, even on a physical level, because if we become arthritic or stiff, we cannot move. (I know this because I had at one time a predisposition to arthritis!)

In this dance we start with our hands back to the left. When the music starts and we turn from facing the center to facing outward, our palms briefly touch in front of our heart (right hand above and caressing the left, then the left palm turns down and the right hand caresses the back of the left hand) after which our arms swing out sideways and float. They float with the undulating movement of the waves, as we take three steps sideways moving counterclockwise around the circle, crossing one foot in front of the other on the second step. Then we swing back around and again the hands come together, with our palms touching. Then the left hand turns over and, as before, the right hand caresses first the palm and then the back of the left hand. We do this as we swing round to face the center again, and, then as before, we take three sideways steps counterclockwise around the circle.

Flowing is internalizing the Love principle. When we are guided by Love, we flow. A rigid person is a person who is not guided by Love. If as a parent we are rigid, we are not truly loving our children. If I as a teacher become rigid, I am not truly loving my students. The qualities of the element of Water are extremely important on every level of life.

In this dance, we start, as in **Everá**, by connecting with the Stream of love through the feeling side of our nature (symbolically the left side). Then we turn around 180 degrees and give out that love with outstretched arms to the world around us. As we do so, we find ourselves supported on the Ocean of Divine Love. Finally, as we turn and swing our hands together, we give ourselves that love—the right (directing) hand caressing first the palm and then the back of the left (nurturing, supporting) hand, the inner masculine within us acknowledging the feminine within—before once again swinging out, turning our attention out 180 degrees and finding ourselves floating on the Ocean of Divine Love.

Movement 20

Overcoming/Conquering

The fourth element is Fire and the next movement is **Overcoming** or **Conquering**. This is a very fiery movement. Fire is often associated with the masculine side. There is a feminine Fire as well, but this dance is a very masculine dance.

It is a dance where we face forward, and it is a dance which strengthens the willpower and the ability to overcome the obstacles of life. In this dance we do not move around from side to side as in **Flowing**. Rather we face steadily forward, keeping our eyes steady and focused on the goal.

Remember that the adversary is not somebody else; the adversary is whatever is holding us back from within. As we go forward round the circle, do not think that the person in front of us is our adversary! Remember we are going forward in a straight line. When we are on a circle, a straight line will take us out to the right of the person in front of us. So we are moving forward, and our eyes should be straight ahead, slightly to the right of the person in front. We keep our eyes, our head, and our shoulders facing forward—fully focused on the goal—as with Zen in the art of archery. In contrast to most other dances of the PanEuRhythmy only our arms and legs swing from side to side—not our body, which resolutely stays facing forward.

Overcoming starts with our arms swinging back to the right-hand side. We have to get that thought in our minds: I am going to overcome. Then the heart follows.

We draw in our energy to the right. We raise the left knee in a very deliberate motion, bending forward from the waist slightly. In this Yin position, we are giving way to our opponent, drawing in his energy, before moving forward to overcome. This pulling back is the first movement, like pulling the string of a bow backwards. We draw our two hands backwards, to our right, slightly below the waist. We lift the left foot off the ground, then step on it, straighten up, and bring the right foot forward, and this time our two hands swing forward and then up, with the palms facing forward. The energy from the palms of the hands is used not so much for healing

73

this time, but for overcoming or surmounting obstacles. For example, if our obstacle is fear, we have to get up and face it. When we face it, we dissolve it.

We then swing our hands back down to the left, and this time we lift the right knee up from the ground. In this, we repeat the action the other way around, this time pulling back to the left before going forward again.

As we swing our arms up, and the palms turn to face forward, it is as if we are shining the light of our inner projector out into the world— making manifest on the screen of life the inner vision and ideals on the filmstrip of our Souls.

Movement 21
Joy of the Earth

We have now gone through four elements: Earth, Air, Water and Fire. The fifth element is Ether. Now ether is an element that scientists used to say did not exist. The ancient scientists talked about ether, and in the Eastern Indian tradition they call it Akasha. Nowadays we talk about the Akashic records, because we have discovered this fifth element does exist. Ether is found in the subtle realm where everything exists not only for a time, but forever. When we utter a sound, when our minds work and speak, the sound goes out into the element of Air, which is the element of the mind. It goes out a certain distance, but as it goes out further from its source, it decreases in power. Eventually it disappears. Yet we are told nothing ultimately ever gets lost. The ripples I cause here go right round through the Ether to affect others on the other side of the planet. They do become lost in the element of Air, but in the element of Ether they are never lost.

The Akashic records consist of the ripples that we put out, not only with our physical words, but with our subtle words—the words that are thought or uttered, the feelings of our hearts. Everything that goes on within ourselves creates ripples in the element of Ether, and those ripples go on forever.

People who can connect with the Akashic records can read the mind and feelings of people through all ages. This is very similar to how radio waves go out into space forever and ever. We have proof; we have spaceships which send messages back even from beyond Neptune. The element of ether is now being recognized. For a while it was too subtle for science to recognize, but science is now rediscovering the spiritual element as well.

Ether is that subtle element in which the creative sound of God begins to descend from the spiritual to the subtle realm (which is the Akasha, the etheric level), before it descends further into the gross physical level.

The first physical level is the level of air, which is invisible. We can feel it but we cannot see it. Fire, Water, and Earth represent the different degrees of subtleness, down to gross materiality.

The element of Ether is the most purely spiritual element, and we reach it by purifying our thoughts and our feelings—all that we put out into the world. We are discovering more and more that what we put out on a subtle level comes back to us personally. That is why we are taught to think positively about everyone and everything, including ourselves, because even our thoughts have an effect.

If you have a project, if you have something you want to do, think about it positively. Write it out on a piece of paper. Do not show it to anybody, but keep it. The thought that you are putting out will gradually materialize, as you keep visualizing and affirming it positively, and working towards it.

We have talked about the symbolism of transmuting the subtle element of Ether, purifying, transforming, and spiritualizing that element. Let me now say a few things about the movement itself. **Joy of the Earth** is a blessing of the Earth. When we have spiritualized and raised all the other four elements, then the Earth can also be in harmony with the subtler dimensions. It can become a paradise once more; it can become Heaven on Earth. Once we have spiritualized the four elements, we can have Heaven on Earth, and mankind can find, as Milton said, "Paradise regained," and so bless all that is, all Nature. The movement of **Joy of the Earth** is a blessing movement. We swing very gently and rhythmically from side to side, picking up our feet and taking little steps around the circle in the counterclockwise direction.

This dance starts with our weight on the right foot, and with our hands to the right. We swing our hands palms downwards left and right, left and right, as if caressing the Earth's aura. I usually visualize myself standing over a field of grain, just letting my hands skim over the ears of corn, like a deva who is blessing the crops.

As we pass our hands to and fro in this way we can feel the energy flowing through the palms of our hands, blessing the Earth. Starting from the right we twice go to the left and to the right. Then we swing round on our right foot and, stepping forward with our left foot, we direct our hands upwards as in **Everá**, palms facing each other, fingers pointing forward and up. We then repeat the movement facing outwards (backs to the center) and again swing our arms four times from side to side (right, left, right, left) and then again forward and up, as we swing back inwards on our left foot to face the center of the circle again, and step on the right foot before repeating the sequence again from the beginning. As Homo sapiens, we have

now entered our true vocation on planet Earth, and are conducting the symphony of life.

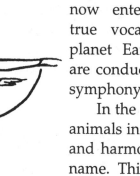

In the Garden of Eden, Adam led the animals in an atmosphere of mutual love and harmony, and he gave them each a name. This function of naming is very important. Naming is giving identity, giving worth, giving respect, giving a function to all that is. So naming the different forms of creation is blessing and giving them each a function. Like the conductor who in turn calls up the strings, the woodwind, and the percussion, so man as a conductor of the physical world is calling up the different parts of the orchestra, and bringing them all into play in a harmonious and concerted way. As the conductor who is conducting the orchestra, in this dance we are blessing and conducting, performing our true functions as human beings, directing towards truth.

Animals will naturally follow human beings who love them, because they look up to man as having a higher consciousness. The animal world is suffering because man is not giving them love and direction. A true master will love and direct an animal, and that animal will be devoted, not only for life, but beyond one lifetime, to that human being.

There is a beautiful account in Richard Bach's book, *A Bridge*

Across Forever, of how, when Richard and Leslie were practicing leaving and re-entering their bodies at will, they saw another spiritual body in their room, and realized it was their cat. They saw the silver cord from the spiritual form of their cat going down to a sleeping cat in the basket. The cat whose subtle body they had recognized with such great joy when they were out of their bodies was the cat which had died a few years before, and they were so glad to be reunited with her! When they looked at the silver cord, however, they realized that the silver cord was connecting her with the cat that lived with them now!

An animal will love beyond death, and will return to its owners. The devotion of an animal is quite incredible, to a master who is truly human. I have been deeply touched by stories of some of the great spiritual men of India, who go out into the Himalayas or the jungle. For instance, Sadhu Sundhar Singh would go out and a leopard would come up to him and even nuzzle his neck against him. People who can make friends with lions and tigers are deeply spiritual people. They do not eat the flesh of animals. They love and respect the animals, and the animals recognize and follow them. At the moment, mankind is doing the opposite—terrorizing and exploiting the animal world, by misusing our superior power and superior consciousness.

Joy of The Earth celebrates the time when the whole earth will rediscover the joy for which it was created, and the song of the angels, "Peace on earth, goodwill towards all" will at last be a reality. Then the animal world and the plant world can once again respect and love their human cousins.

I once had neighbors who loved animals and who rescued and brought up a pigeon that had fallen out of its nest. The pigeon became so unafraid that it would come into all our homes, and they had to protect the pigeon at night from the cats and dogs who wanted to leap on it and eat it up, because it was so trusting. Of course when the earth returns to being a paradise, then "the wolf shall dwell with the lamb; and the calf and the young lion together; and a little child shall lead them."[1]

As a child, those words from Isaiah always touched me deeply, but, in the then context of World War II, seemed impossibly

---

1. Isaiah 11:6

idealistic. Yet they always resonated in my heart. Now it moves me to tears to see how they are actually coming true in the world today—with the prayers of so many and the quiet, dedicated work over half a century of the United Nations.

"They shall beat their swords into plowshares and their spears into pruning hooks: nation shall not lift up sword against nation, neither shall they learn war any more.[1] They shall not hurt nor destroy.... for the earth shall be filled with the knowledge of God, as the waters cover the sea."[2]

---

1. Isaiah 2:4
2. Isaiah 11:9

Peter Deunov meditating by the Seven Sacred Lakes.

Section IV

Working in Partnership

The last five dances of the PanEuRhythmy, before the two concluding movements, **Singing and Breathing** and the final **Blessing**, are dances of Partnership. They represent that stage in our spiritual evolution when we are mature enough to work in perfect harmony with another being to accomplish the task of bringing on earth the Kingdom of Heaven—"Paradise regained," to quote Milton.

The dances progress through the stages of Partnership that we often associate with marriage, that most challenging of all partnerships: from the joyful exhilaration of the early stages of becoming acquainted; through the commitment to step out together and link and harmonize at every level of our being; through the rapturous moments of celebrating how happy we are that the partnership is working; on through the long haul of persevering through all difficult and arid parts of our long journey together; 'till we reach the grand finale of our triumphant Homecoming, acclaimed by the host of unseen witnesses cheering us on and waiting to receive us into the subtler realms of being awaiting us on completion of our life's journey.

What it means to have been in the Mountains

"Have you climbed the mountain lately?" My fine arts coordinator always asked me this, and now I can say, truly, I have.

I had never been to a non-English-speaking country. Though I love being out of doors, the long trek and the rocky climb filled me with apprehension. Much about the trip to the Rila Mountains gave me pause.

And yet, I felt clearly called to go there. Since meeting Ardella two years before, my passion and love for the PanEuRhythmy and the teachings of Peter Deunov grew and grew, supported by our St. Louis PanEuRhythmy community—for such our dance group had become. I put aside my own concerns—physical, financial, emotional—and embarked on this spiritual journey.

Oh! Imagine how I felt that very first day, winded from the climb to the Lake of Purity and arriving just as the musicians struck their chords, when I was pulled immediately into the vortex of the dance! Mists were rising from the surrounding mountains, as hundreds of us moved together in profound silence out of which the music—the beautiful music—arose. In that moment, I stepped into the Eternal Dance.

The days in the mountains held glories—chopping vegetables, singing beautiful songs, wise teachers, gentle healers, and chief among them, dancing the Dance itself—PanEuRhythmy, The Sunbeams, The Pentagram. In our little camp, a community of people from all over the world—Mauritius, Australia, the United States, England, Ireland, France, Bulgaria—I found great connectedness, profound silence, unity of spirit. I was tested in every way—and nurtured, and served, and loved.

My return finds me more active physically, daily performing the morning exercises, more deeply quiet, listening for the music and moving with my partners in life. I now know it is possible to be the sunshine moment by moment. I have danced the Dance. I have climbed the Mountain.

Phyllis Thorpe
Teacher, director of theatre and communication.
Christmas Day 1996

Movement 22
Friendship

These last five dances are some of the most beautiful dances because they are like the culmination of the PanEuRhythmy. We have now reached the point, symbolically, in our spiritual evolution, where we are ready to enter into a very fine, high level of partnership. Up until now we've been dancing side-by-side, each working on our own evolution, being aware of our partner but not actually connecting. Now, for the first time, we turn to face our partner.

We have passed through this wonderful stage of bringing back the Kingdom of Heaven on earth, recreating the Garden of Eden, Paradise on Earth, and now we can move on to work in partnerships and get to know one another as truly Divine beings. We have risen to our full stature, to the high calling of each one of us, because each of us is not just a simple little incarnate human being, but a very great soul. In India they have the expression "Mahatma" for somebody who has fully manifested, or very largely manifested his true greatness. "Maha" means great, and "Atma" means spirit or soul. "Atma" comes from the word for breathing,[1] because the spirit is the breath of life. So somebody who truly realizes his soul's potential is a "Great Soul." That is why Gandhi was called Mahatma Gandhi, because he realized his divine purpose. The joy of discovering someone else who has also realized his or her divine purpose, and the joy of meeting and working with such people is quite extraordinary.

In this next dance, **Friendship**, one partner faces outward in the circle and the other inward. We clasp both of our partner's hands, always with the right hand above and the left hand below, and we look into each

---

1. In German, "Atmen" means "Breathing."

other's eyes. There we connect with the Divine essence, that Divine potential in the other, which is, to a greater or lesser extent,

manifest, and we love and recognize that Divine being in our partner. We swing back and forward, then let go of our partner's hands as we swing around and out. Our hands move to our heart center briefly and then our arms swing open and out, opening our hearts in gratitude; we look up and give thanks to the heavens for the joy of friendship and of meeting such another wonderful being, and we share our love and joy with all.

Our hands then swing back and join, and then together they swing forward and around, as we swing back around and join hands with our partner again. Then together we swing forwards, backwards, forwards, and out and round again.

Each time as we link up with our partner we look into their eyes. We recognize and respond to that divine being that is shining through their eyes, the windows of the soul. As we swing out again, our arms open in a gesture of thanksgiving and sheer joy. We give thanks to the heavens for the beauty of this friendship. We swing out to share that joy and beauty with the whole world, then we bring it back into our hearts as we join our hands, clasping our palms together, to swing back and link with our partner again.

There are three parts to this dance. First we link hands with our partners to form a circuit of energy, moving down our right arms and up our left and through our hearts to our right hand again. Next we let go and allow this circuit to move out through the whole universe, recognizing the oneness of that love-energy flowing through all that is. Finally, we clasp our own hands together, and experience that circuit of love flowing through our own being and the fullness of our own self-love, out of which we can then turn to love our partners again—and once more experience together the Divine flow of love.

This dance follows on naturally from the last five, for when we have fulfilled our function of guiding and directing all the levels of nature, the animal and the plant kingdoms, and we are in tune with the angelic realms, we can at last find one another in Paradise, and move on together to enact in perfect harmony the Divine plan of creating Heaven on Earth.

Peter Deunov.

Movement 23

A Beautiful Day

We move now into the second dance of the partnership dances. In the previous dance, **Getting Acquainted**, we for the first time connected with our partners. And this is a little bit like falling in love. You suddenly look at the person and realize what a Divine, splendid, wonderful being is in your partner. And you see that

Light in their eyes and you feel that heart connection with them. And then you turn out and open wide the portals of your heart, opening to the whole world and sharing that Light and that Love.

Then in this dance, as we move forward into **A Beautiful Day**, we are moving forward to work together in partnership. We are starting off on a beautiful day.

This dance is in four parts. We begin with our hands on our hips because we're focusing on our lower body, on our lower chakras, and getting them into harmony and balance. And so, we raise the right knee and, standing on the left leg and bending the left knee, we bounce down and up three times on the left leg before stepping down on the right foot. We're finding that delicate balance within our own being. In order to keep the right knee up, the right leg relaxed, and bend with the left knee, one has to be in a very delicate inner state of balance.

The PanEuRhythmy up to now has been bringing us into that balance. Now, in our partnership, we're finding that inner balance, first on the left leg and then on the right leg. The left leg symbolizes our feeling nature and the right leg our thinking nature, so we're finding that inner balance within ourselves between our thinking and our feeling.

In the second part of the dance we bring that balance up to the upper body, the upper chakras, by including the arms in the

movement. For the first part of the dance we were just using our legs. Now we also use our arms. We raise our right hand along with our right knee, until we're balancing on the left leg, with the right hand and the right knee raised. The feeling side of our nature is supporting and balancing, giving that little bounce, that little rhythm to allow the thinking side of our nature to really manifest in the world. And then the right hand swings down and the left hand swings up along with the left knee, and we balance this time on the right leg. That's the second part of the dance, and so far we're not yet actually holding hands with our partner.

Only when we come to the third part of the dance do we physically connect with our partner. We take hold of our partner's hand, the right hand over the left, because the left hand is the

supportive or receiving hand and the right hand the giving hand. The outer hand is on our hip and now, in harmony and in rhythm with our partner, we raise the right knee and balance on the left leg and three times bounce on the left leg, with the toes of the right foot just above the ground, before stepping down onto the right foot. We then go through the same movements again, but this time with our left knee raised. We're now finding that inner balance within the partnership.

The fourth and final part of this dance is creating something beautiful for God in the partnership. We're all working on creating something beautiful for God in our own lives; now we are doing it together with our partner. Here we see the intimate connection in the partnership, as we need to be inwardly poised both in our own inner balance and in the mutual balance with our partner.

As you can see there is a delicate balance between the two partners. The outer partners are lifting their right arms and right legs together. The inner partners are lifting their outer arms (their left arms) along with their right legs. This movement of the inner partners is a more feminine movement. Women move more from the waist, so in this movement you are turning your upper and lower body in opposite directions, pivoting at the waist. The person on the outside has a more masculine movement in that the whole body moves together, so the right arm and the right leg come up together (then the left arm and the left leg together).

When performed with poise and grace, this is a very beautiful movement, and symbolizes the beauty of truly harmonious partnership in a great enterprise.

The movement of the arms can be very majestic and graceful. As the right feet step forward, the outer arms sweep out from the body and up, arching high as a Gothic arch over our heads to connect with our partner's outer hand. Meanwhile, the inner hands let go—symbolizing letting go of our need to hold on to each other for support, and trusting that the Universe will support us as we together create this Gothic beauty.

As we then let go of our outer hands clasped over our heads, we stretch our arms up and out as they gracefully swing down to our (outer) sides again. As our left feet move forward, our inner hands connect, and, bending our elbows, we bring our hands up to shoulder level—symbolically forming again that intimate physical connection between us, which balances and strengthens the outer spiritual endeavor we are engaged in together. As the music comes to an end, our feet come together, and we continue to hold hands above our heads for just a moment longer.

Movement 24

How Happy We Are!

Now I want to move on to the third of the five partnership dances. In this dance we are celebrating how happy we are that our partnership is working. This dance, **How Happy We Are!**, is based on an old Bulgarian courtship dance, "Ratshenitsa," which was in a minor key. As a result of the Bulgarians being oppressed by the Turks for five hundred years, their music tended to have a sad, nostalgic tone. Peter Deunov said it was very important to change this sadness into joy and to let go of suffering. We've been through centuries of suffering, and suffering, he said, has been our main teacher, but now we are moving out of the age of suffering. We can be thankful for the suffering we've been through; suffering has been like the scourge, like the stick that has woken up the donkey and got it moving, but let's be thankful for the suffering and let it go. We don't have to hold onto it any more. Now that we're awake and our hearts are opening to love we can respond, and love can be our teacher.

We are moving forward now into a new age of harmony and joy. We can see this in the world all around us at the moment. In South Africa the blacks and the whites are getting together, setting up a government together. The Israelis and the Arabs are beginning to find ways to live together. Hopefully in Northern Ireland the Catholics and the Protestants will soon overcome their differences. Recently I spent the day with two Russians who had come "from Russia with love." And now so many Americans are going, with love, over to Russia. We're living in an exciting time, when all the conflicting parts of the world are coming together in love and harmony. We're all finding a new harmony together, and that is what we are celebrating in this dance.

We start with our hands on our hips, and bouncing on each step (as if it were two steps) we take three steps forward and rock back on our left foot for the fourth step. The little bounces are expressive of the love and joy that we're feeling.

For every two or three steps forward in life there's a step back; it is normal and natural. We make a few steps and progress forward in our lives and then we've got to go back and recap or re-evaluate ourselves, to strengthen where we've come from.

Then we change after the fourth step back. We let our hands swing loosely down, take our partner's hand, and then swing both hands forward and up as we take two steps forward and then swing both arms back, as we take one step back. We repeat this step four times. After the fourth time we release our partner's hand and put our hands on our hips again and repeat the three steps forward and one back.

This dance is in four parts. The first part is three steps forward and one back four times. The second part is holding hands and taking two steps forward, swinging the arms forward and up, then one step back, repeated four times. The third and fourth parts are a repetition of the first and second parts.

This is a very joyful, exhilarating dance, and—if we really throw ourselves into it—it leaves us really

celebrating "How happy we are!"

Movement 25

Step-By-Step

The fourth dance in the Partnership series is called **Step-by-Step**. This dance is teaching us about the step-by-step process of completing the long journey of life. Now we have experienced the joy of getting to know each other, then the exhilaration of the honeymoon, we have to move on "step-by-step." We have to take life step-by-step, being in the "here and now." There are times of rejoicing when we see the big vision, but we can only accomplish the vision when we live it step-by-step. It's not that we've bitten off more than we can chew. You can eat an elephant, but only one bite at a time. So in this movement we learn about being very centered, and taking life "step-by-step."

Peter Deunov said that in this dance we're strengthening our nervous system. We're finding an inward strength and centeredness within our being. We're conducting the solar energies into the earth and the earth energies back up to the sun. Our bodies are like trees, conducting the energies of Heaven and Earth so that a blending can take place. This is the function of human beings and also of trees. As step out, we open up to the solar energies, directing them into the earth, and when our feet come together we're connecting with the energies of the earth and directing them heavenward.

In this dance you will find the music is very picturesque. The music has a soulful quality; it is like the soul's yearning for our heavenly home, wanting to complete our pilgrimage, to complete what we came into this world to do. We're wanting to perfect the picture we came to paint or the statue we came to sculpt in this world. And we have to go at it step-by-step. If a sculptor is for one moment distracted he can chip the wrong bit off the block, and then the whole statue is destroyed. So in life we've got to go step-by-step. It's so easy to chip off the wrong part of the statue. With our lives we're sculpting this beautiful gift that we're leaving to the world, and we want to have it perfect and complete. So we have to bring full attention to every detail, every step.

The music has a soulful, yearning, dancing quality; it's almost like our heart and soul are dancing with the angels, yet our feet have to connect with the ground. Sometimes I find that one can almost be distracted by the music. It's like our heads are so much in the clouds that we forget the movement of our feet. Because this dance is very simple it is very easy to lose our place in the dance. This serves as a constant reminder to stay grounded, to stay with the movement of our feet even while our soul is listening to the heavenly music. This is a reminder to keep our connection both with the heavenly music and with the Earth.

In this dance we are reminded of the interdependence of an orchestra. The bass and the percussion, by keeping the grounded rhythm going, bring out more fully the beautiful music of the violins, the oboes, the flutes, and so on. Whatever instrument you're playing (in the orchestra) you have to listen to all the others as well. The same applies to ourselves; whether our consciousness is in our soul, or in our eyes, ears, or feet, we have to also keep it in the moment. It's a matter of staying aware of the two extremities; it's important to be grounded, but it's also important to hear the "distant drummer," to hear the heavenly music inspired by the heavenly vision. Otherwise, as the saying goes, "without Vision, the people perish." Unless we have that

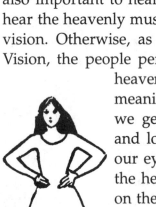

heavenly vision, life loses its meaning, loses its purpose, and we get depressed or disoriented and lose our strength, our goal. We have to keep our eye on the heavenly goal, our ears attuned to the heavenly music, and also have our feet firmly on the ground. This is the challenge of human life, if we are going to live it to the fullest.

In this dance we have to be very centered. We're going to stand on our left leg and this time the left knee will stay straight. In this dance, we will not bounce. We keep our hands on our hips throughout. The right leg goes out sideways, toes pointed, and we touch the ground with the toes of our right foot and then bring the feet back together.

We begin the first sequence in this dance by leading with the right foot: out to the right then together (twice), forward then together (twice), and then three steps forward: right, left, right, and complete by bringing our feet together.

The next sequence is the same thing, only this time leading with the left foot: out to the left, back together (twice), forward, then back together (twice), and then three steps forward: left, right, left, and complete by bringing our feet together. Make sure you bring your feet together; it's very easy to swing one's feet back so that you're actually stepping forward and back, which is incorrect.

As you dance keep your eyes forward and up, at least horizontal or a little bit higher. It is not necessary to look at our feet because, as the Native Americans say, we do have "eyes in our feet" or "eyes in the tips of our toes."

These "eyes in the tips of our toes" are the eyes of the body and can see the way forward; we can allow the lower part of the body to find its own way. The eyes in the head are the windows of the Soul and need to be looking up and ahead, and the ears listening to the heavenly music. As we dance let us take in the feast of nature around us. With our ears we take in the singing of the birds, the sound of the breeze rustling through the trees, and the sound of the Silence permeating all space. Take in the sights and sounds of Nature, because our spirits are fed from the higher source while our feet are doing their work on the ground. This, in a way, is a parable of Life. We need to constantly allow our souls to be fed from above, keep open to the heavenly manna so that with the physical part of our being we can carry out our part in the Divine plan on Earth.

Step-by-Step is a little like "court dancing." We move tall and stately and avoid looking at our feet. In these last few dances we do a lot with the feet, and it's very easy to have our eyes constantly on our feet. We need to keep our head up, our eyes looking forward and up, and remember that our feet can look after themselves. We need to keep the feet relaxed and move with the thighs, allowing the lower leg and foot to drop to the ground in a very easy way—toes connecting first and feeling out the ground, before we touch the ground with the ball of the foot, then the heel, and shift the weight of the body by degrees onto that foot. There is a part of our consciousness that knows exactly what our feet are doing without our eyes having to check on them. By doing this we are expanding our vision and opening beyond what the physical eyes can see, thereby increasing our peripheral vision.

In truth what you are doing is slipping out of physical seeing into clairvoyant seeing, the super-sensory seeing, because there's a sense in which, if you can really open up your vision, you can see all around you, even behind, above, and below. People who are clairvoyant say that clairvoyance usually comes with the peripheral vision. As soon as they look directly at, say, an angel or a fairy, they don't see it any more. They only see them out of the corner of their eye. People who see auras don't look directly at the person. They look to one side, and then they see the person's aura with their peripheral vision.

Movement 26
Bright and Early

This dance is the grand finale. It's like we've gone step-by-step through life, we've almost crossed the desert, and we're now coming to the promised land. As we come into the promised land it's like the end of one lifetime or one life cycle. Many people, when dying or moving on in some way, get that sense of the invisible cloud—or crowd—of witnesses who are applauding and leading us on. There is a story in the Bible of the children of Israel once feeling totally overwhelmed by the enemy, because they were few in number and they were surrounded by hundreds of their enemies. They thought that they were going to be defeated. The prophet prayed and the voice of an angel said, "Look around you. Those who are with you are far more in number than those who are against you." When the prophet opened his eyes and looked around, all around them he saw hundreds and hundreds of angels, all armed with flaming swords. Suddenly he realized that there was no way they could lose the battle. And sure enough, even though they were only a small group, they won the battle.

That, in a way, is a parable for what is happening in our lives. There are times in our lives when we feel as if we are overwhelmed by tremendous odds. When the odds seem overwhelming, let us just remember that vision of the prophet, that those who are with us are far greater than those who are against us. We all have physical, material problems in our lives, but actually the hosts of angels, the hosts of unseen witnesses around us, far outnumber the physical problems. Though we may think we're at the end of our resources, we're not. These heavenly hosts can regenerate our body and energy so that we're able to move on to a higher level of being.

In this dance we move forward together with our partner and in a beautiful, stately dance. This dance is in three parts with six steps in each of the first two parts. With our hands on our hips, we swing the right leg twice around the left, forward and back, forward and back, with toes pointing and touching the ground at each end of the swing. We then take four steps forward, finishing with the feet together—right, left, right, together. Next we swing the left leg around the right, forward and back, forward and back, again touching the ground with toes pointed at each end of the swing. We again follow this with four steps forward, this time leading with the left leg, and bringing the feet together on the last step—left, right, left, together.

In the second part of the dance, elbows bent, we hold inner hands with our partner, up at eye or shoulder level, with the outer hands on our hips. We lead with the right foot for four steps, taking tiny steps. Then we swing our inner hands back and forwards, back and forwards, shifting our weight onto our heels, then onto our toes, twice each. This sequence is performed six times.

In the third section of this dance we let go of our partner's hand, and place both hands on our hips and take four little transition steps forward to move slightly out from our partner. Now, with sufficient clearance

for extended arms, we repeat the movements of the feet in the previous dance **Step-by-Step** (right foot out to the right, feet together (twice), right foot forward and back together (twice), then four steps forward, ending with the feet together) but this time we will add arm movements to coordinate with the movements of our feet. As our foot steps out

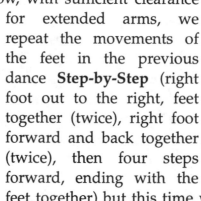

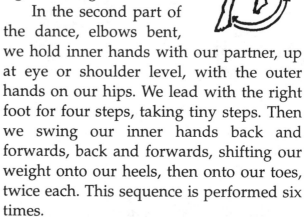

sideways, we extend both hands out horizontally from our shoulders. Our hands come back down to our hips as our foot comes back to join the other. When we extend our foot forward, we extend our arms out in front of us horizontally from the shoulders (palms facing down), then again bring them down to our waist, as our feet come together.

This final part of the dance forms an exhilarating crescendo of energy, which brings the PanEuRhythmy to a grand climax. There is a sense of picking up the themes of the previous dances and weaving them all together into a joyful grand finale. As the energy and emotion build up, it is like a stirring, profoundly joyful and triumphal Homecoming.

Movement 27
Singing and Breathing

The next movement is **Singing and Breathing**. Here, finally, while standing still and facing each other in the circle, we break into song. As we come to the end of our "journey," we express to our friends and companions the joy we feel.

We open our hearts in love at the initial chord as we take a deep breath in, swing our arms out from the heart forward in a horizontal arc, ending with our arms straight out from our shoulders, with the palms facing forward. Then, with the music we sing "Ah"—that

sound of fullness of awe and joyful wonder—our arms sweeping slowly back in a large, horizontal arc forward and around until our fingers touch our heart at the last note. This is repeated nine times, singing three times up the scale, three times down the scale, and finally the last three times, taking an extra deep breath and singing three notes up the scale, seven notes down and three notes up again.

This **Singing and Breathing** brings the energy built up in the PanEuRhythmy to a quieter and finer level of being, taking us inward into a subtler state of meditation. It enables us to open our hearts to one another and to the world, and to become more fully aware of the Joy and the Grace we share. It literally enables our hearts to sing.

Movement 28
The Blessing

Finally, in the last movement, **The Blessing**, we encompass all that vastness we have experienced. We center it into our bodies, so that it stays with us as we move into the day and out into the world and we go about our tasks, taking with us that energy and joy and inspiration and insight.

We remain in our circle, facing the center with our arms loosely down by our sides. We then turn our palms to face outwards and slowly breathe in as we raise our arms out, sideways and up until our fingers touch above our heads. This signifies connecting with the oneness of Spirit. We start exhaling as we lower our hands, slowly, to within a few inches from the top of our heads. Our hands then separate as we enter the world of duality (in the physical) and travel down, palms facing our bodies,  a few inches away from our bodies, down the front of the two sides of our body until our arms once again hang loosely by our sides. As we make this downward movement we bring the oneness of Spirit into the duality of our incarnate nature. As our hands hang by our sides, the energy continues to travel down through our fingers, down our legs, and meets under our feet, thus containing our aura.

As we make this sweeping gesture, around and up and down our bodies, we say together the final blessing, "May the Peace of God .... and the Pure Joy of God .... Live in our Hearts Forever." The exact translation from the Bulgarian is, "May the Peace of God abide .... and may Divine Joy and Gladness .... Arise in our Hearts." And we could also simply say, "May Love, Peace and Joy .... Live in our Hearts Forever."

Peter Deunov.

Section V

The Music and Lyrics

The music and lyrics in this section are presented by Vessela Nestorova and Barnaby Brown. The wondrous movements of the PanEuRhythmy are complemented by extraordinary music and inspiring words.

The Music and Lyrics

Everyone should sing the PanEuRhythmy! How many of us have become silent birds in a hostile wood where only an occasional nightingale sings out? Performing the PanEuRhythmy brings spring to the spirit, helping even the most reticent humans burst into song. If you have been deprived of the wholesome natural tonic of your own voice, then let the PanEuRhythmy restore it to you. Your song is sure to sound worse than some, better than others, but in any case sure to write a smile on your heart.

Singing the PanEuRhythmy in a comprehensible language has the advantage of shedding light on the movements as they are performed, bringing idea and action immediately into correspondence. The original Bulgarian lyrics remain the international standard, however, and English speakers who would rather be at one with their foreign counterparts should give priority to learning them. The extra effort this requires is rewarded by the pure resonances of the Bulgarian language which, like Italian, is more beautiful to sing than English. Nonetheless, the English lyrics are felt to be of service in the early stages of learning the movements and to be of great pleasure beyond, so are provided here.

Acknowledgments

The following pages of music and lyrics could not have appeared without the wonderful hospitality poured on me while working in Bulgaria, the constant enthusiasm of my mother Alison, and the manifold assistance of PanEuRhythmy teachers the world over. Suggestions on how best to represent the music on paper have been gratefully received from numerous quarters; in particular, I thank Peter Ganev and Joanna Strateva for giving generously of their expertise. Above all, however, this work owes its existence to the fountain of wisdom, joy, and creativity that is Vessela Nestorova.

Barnaby Brown
Sofia, March 1997

I

1.-10. The First Day of Spring

Outward gestures synchronize with the right foot throughout.

1. Awakening, 9. Purification

Moderato (♩. = 60)

Voice*

1. Rise!   A - wak - en!   Spring   is   here.
9. On   the __ breath   of   God   we   rise

O - pen your door   to   day - light   clear.
through - all __ clouds   and   stor - my   skies,

Full - ness of   life   for   ev - ery - thing
pu - ri - fied   if,   come   what   may,

brings   the __ first   bright   day   of   spring,
sow - ing __ beau - ty   is   our   way,

brings   the __ first   bright   day   of   spring.
sow - ing __ beau - ty   is   our   way.

2. Reconciliation, 10. Flying

2. Na - ture is smi - ling,   sun   is __ shi - ning,   hea - vens are blue,
10. Fly - ing,   soar - ing,   sun - shine_ pour - ing   in   and_ through

wa - ken - ing earth   to   life   a - new.
ev - ery __ cell,   we're   born   a - new.

* Any part of the melody may be sung an octave higher or lower so that it lies more comfortably in the voice.
An edition for violinists and other instrumentalists is published separately.

35

Flo - wers, trees and birds and bees, in

39

co - lours_ bright and voi - ces_ clear,

43

ce - le - brate the spring that's here,

47

ce - le - brate the spring that's here. Fine

3. Giving

51

3. Now be o - pen to re - ceive

55

all the bless - ings spring days _ leave,

59

beau - ti - ful gifts of life, thoughts bright and pure, ____

65

feel - ings sure, feel-ings of love that will en - dure, ____

72

thoughts _ as rays of sun - shine in the spring. ____

78

Gifts_ of gold this glad time now to us will bring. ____

4. Ascending   ossia:

right arm with right foot

4. Then look up at yon - der — sun and hail his— work of ——

won - der done. Sing your praise un - to the skies, a

joy - ful spar - kle in your eyes. Feel the sac - red

left arm up

thrill! —— With the birds the air with mu - sic fill. ——

5. Elevation

both up   both down

5. *High - er, ev - er high - er   ev - ery-one as - pire.* ——

Ne - ver think to stop   un - til   you— reach   the

hands on hips

most   ex - alt - ed   moun - tain   top. ——

6. Opening, 7. Liberation, 8. Clapping

6. right hand opens
7 & 8. fists tear apart   8. clap   8. clap

6. Cast   off the clothes   of the cold   win - ter - time,
7. Fi - nal - ly, freed   from the chains   of the past,
8. Joy   like a spring   from the heart   let — flow!

128

bathe   in the   rays   of   to - day's   sun - shine.
break - ing a - way,   li - ber - at - ed   at   last,
In   ev - ery - thing   is   new   life   a - glow.

132   * 3

Deep - ly __ breathe, ab - sorb - ing ___ all   in __ sight,
fly   o - ver lakes   to   moun - tain __ peaks sno-wy white;
Share the _ joy,   the   soar - ing ___ of   the _ soul;

137

thank - ing _ God   for the free - dom and joy   of __ light. ___
there, at the door - step of God, fold your wings and a - light. ___
bless   ev-ery-one   on your way; give your love to __ all. ___

143   6. left hand opens (with right foot)   * 3

Shin - ing a - bove,   the   sun   shows _ us   the _ way,
Blessed is the soul   that, one   with __ God, at - tains
Sing - ing the song   of   free - dom, _ clap your _ hands,

148   3

fill - ing our hearts with _ joy   this _ spring - time __ day,
life   ev - er - last - ing, _ life on __ high - er ___ planes,
send - ing _ rays   of __ joy   to __ far - thest _ lands,

153   * 3

shin - ing a - bove,   the   sun   shows _ us   the _ way,
blessed is the soul   that, one   with __ God, at - tains
sing - ing the song   of   free - dom, _ clap your _ hands,

158   3

fill - ing our hearts with _ joy   this spring - time _ day. ___
life   ev - er - last - ing, _ life on _ high - er ___ planes. __
send _ ing _ rays   of __ joy   to __ far - thest _ lands. ___

D.C.
for
verses
9. & 10.

* ossia:

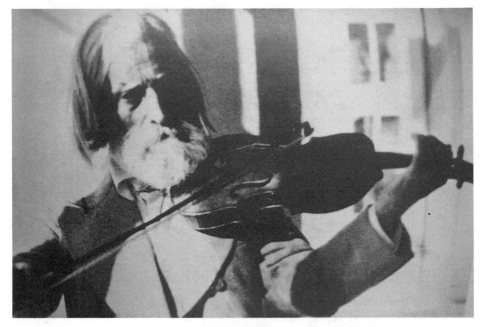

Peter Deunov playing the violin.

11. Everà

Allegretto grazioso (♩. = 62)

right   forward   back   left   forward

1. Dance in the dawn, dance on the green and spark - ling,
2. Dance in the dawn, wel - come the ri - sing sun with

back   etc.

decked with dew - drops lawn; af - ter a night of rest ____ a -
hap - pi - ness and song; join in the har - mo - ny ____ of

- gain in light_ be dressed. ____ *Breathe the mor - ning air; ____*
na - ture's dan - cing throng. ____

let the bree - zes waft a - way your care; ____

rhyth-mic-'ly dance with brooks and flo - wers fra - grant, fair; ____

grace - ful and free, step light - ly on your way ____

on this in - spir - ing bright spring day. ____

12. Jumping

The hands spring apart immediately upon clapping to
resume their opening position: palms forward, arms upstretched.

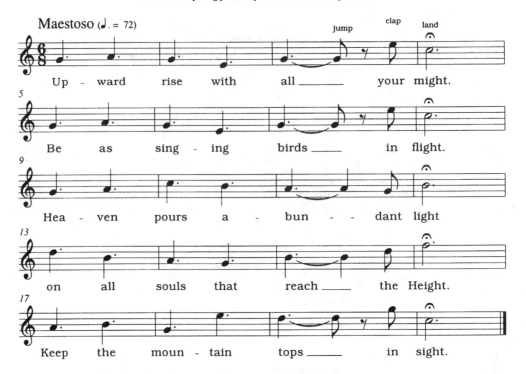

Up - ward   rise   with   all _____   your might.

Be   as   sing - ing   birds _____   in   flight.

Hea - ven   pours   a - bun - - dant   light

on   all   souls   that   reach _____   the Height.

Keep   the   moun - tain   tops _____   in   sight.

13. Weaving

The partner (initially) on the right takes two steps forward and remains in front throughout.
Only when weaving from left to right does the left foot begin, crossing over the right on the strong beat.

Day   by day,   hour   by hour   weav - ing   on   life's   loom _____

thoughts di - vine,   feel - ings fine   com - ing   in - to   bloom; ___

for   the new   Light   and Love   now pre - pare we   am - ple   room.

13
E - very day   think and say that Light will come to - mor - row;

17
Love is now   on its way to   ba - nish fear and   woe;

21
so   we work   and we pray for   bright - er thoughts to know.

25
Weav - ing thus we   take and give   na - ture's gifts di - vine, ____

29
learn - ing dai - ly how to live   high - er lives sub - lime; ____

33
weav - ing thus we   all re - ceive the bles - sings of this time.

37
Day   by day,   hour by hour weav - ing on life's   loom ____

41
thoughts di - vine and feel - ings fine,   for the new life mak - ing room,

45
for the life which turns the night to   day and lights our up - ward way.

14. Thinking

Begin up to the right. The slowly descending arc is gracefully paced.

Lento, ad libitum (♩ = c 52)

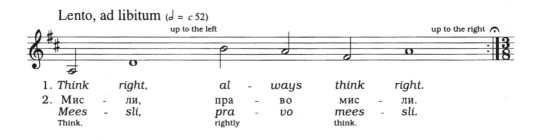

up to the left   up to the right

1. *Think   right,   al - ways   think   right.*
2. Мис - ли,   пра - во   мис - ли.
   Mees - sli,   pra - vo   mees - sli.
   Think.   rightly   think.

Allegretto (♩. = 66)

circling

Sus - tain most sac - red thoughts of   life   that   ra - diate light,
Све - ще - ни   мис - ли   за   жи - во - та   ти   кре - пи,
Sve - shte - ni mees - sli   za   ji - vo - ta   ti   kre - pi,
Sacred   thoughts   of   life   you   sustain.

sus - tain most sac - red thoughts of   life   that   ra - diate   light.____
све - ще - ни   мис - ли   за   жи - во - та   ти   кре - пи,____
sve - shte - ni mees - sli   za   ji - vo - ta   ti   kre - pi,____

3 outward pushes   circling

Sus - tain,   sus - tain,   sus - tain,   sus - tain   most
кре - пи,   кре - пи,   кре - пи,   све - ще   ни
kre - pi,   kre - pi,   kre - pi,   sve - shte - ni

sac - red thoughts of   life   that   ra - diate   light. _____
мис - ли   за   жи - во - та   ти   кре - пи. _____
mees - sli   za   ji - vo - ta   ti   kre - pi. _____

15. Aoum

Lento (♩ = 48)   (4 times)

А - ум,   А - ум,   А - ум, ___ Ом, ___ Ом, ___ Ау - мен.
A - oum,   A - oum,   A - oum, ___ *Om,* ___ *Om,* ___ *Aou - men.*

16. The Rising Sun

Adagio (♩ = 80)

1. *Be - hold   the   ris - ing   sun,   send - ing   glo - rious   light,*
2. Из - гря - ва   слън - це - то,   пра - ща   свет - ли - на,
   Iz - grya - va   slun - tse - to,   pra - shta   svet - li - na,
   Rising is   the sun.   it is sending   light.

fil - ling   life   with   joy   and   pure   de - light.
но - си   ра - дост   за   жи - во - та   тя.
nos - si   ra - dost   za   ji - vo - ta   tya.
bringing   joy   to   life   it is.

Moderato (♩ = 80)

6. then 7 cupping motions. bubbling up the sides of the body from thighs to ribcage

Feel   the   liv - ing   spring - ing   po - wer   flow - ing,
Си - ла   жи - ва   из - вор - на   те - чу - ща,
Si - la   ji - va   iz - vor - na   te - choo - shta,
Power   living   springing   is flowing.

(2nd time) hands to chest

feel   the   liv - ing   spring - ing   po - wer   flow - ing. ___
си - ла   жи - ва   из - вор - на   те - чу - ща. ___
si - la   ji - va   iz - vor - na   te - choo - shta. ___

Give with the right foot. receive with the left.

Зун ме - зун, ___   зун ме - зун ___ би - ном ту ме - то. ___
Zoon me - zoon, ___   *zoon me - zoon* ___ *bi - nom too me - to.* ___
[no translation]

17. The Square

Moderato (♩. = 60)

right out   together   left out   together

1. Bright is the morn, _____ filled with the frag - rance
2. Red is the east, _____ God's lov - ing lips its

sweet of flo - wers just born; white pearls of dew, a
bril - liant fore - head have kissed, fil - ling the mor - ning

gold - en crown her glo - rious head a - dorn. _____
air with vib - rant life and sac - red bliss. _____

All na - ture sings! _____ All na - ture now with mu - sic

rings, _____ prais - ing the dawn, _____ prais - ing the

mor - ning new - ly born, _____ prais-ing the ris - ing

sun, the ra - diant fa - ther of the morn. _____

18. Beauty & 19. Flowing

18. Take 2 steps forward for every 1 back.

19. Take 4 steps forward for every 1 back. The left hand (upturned) receives the right every time.
fingers face to face and parallel. As the body turns, the hands glide apart and the left turns face downward.
The right hand then strokes the back of the left from wrist to fingertips as the arms spread out to 'fly'.

20. Overcoming

Eyes and shoulders unwaveringly forward

"Night - time is o - ver!" says the sun;

like - wise is sad - ness o - ver - come.

Stea - di - ly for - ward we brave - ly press,

through days of hap - pi - ness, through dis - tress.

Life is end - less love and beau - ty,

and to do God's will our du - ty,

life is end - less love and beau - ty,

and to do God's will our du - ty.

21. Joy of the Earth

Toes lifting, moving ever slightly forward

Build a new home where Joy can ___ live,
build it of mu - sic an - gels ___ give,
build it of Pu - ri - ty, build it of Light,
make it a pa - lace ___ large and ___ white.
Let its win - dows ___ o - pen wide
wel - come in the ___ mor - ning light:
Joy will ___ come, that love - ly queen;
rea - di - ly she will en - ter ___ in.

Now with mu - sic work be - gin.

Build with glad - ness, build in the spring - time

mor - ning; as in hea - ven,

sun - light your home a - dorn - - ing,

through ev - ery win - dow pour - - ing.

Slow - ly ris - ing, Hea - ven's hand in your

la - bour, rea - dy to share with your neigh - bor,

this home of Joy Di - vine,

beau - tif' - ly flood - ed with sun - - shine,

shall be for - e - ver thine.

22. Friendship

As the arms spread out to 'fly' the fingertips momentarily touch, palms down.
After 'flying', whichever arm is forward swings back to join the other in an extended ellipse, raised to the rear:
in both cases the right hand turns face out to meet the left (which faces into the shoulder), fingers face to face and parallel.
With the next forward step, the hands glide apart as they pass below the chest,
leaving upturned left and downturned right ready to take your partner's hands.

Allegretto grazioso (♩. = 62)

swing apart   *fly*   *ellipse to the rear*   *turn together*   *swing forwards*   *back*   *etc.*

1. Touch of the hand   is   bles-sing a friend, through
2. Кол - ко при - ят - но   пти - чен - це пе - е
    Kol - ko pri - at - no   ptit-chen-tse pe - e
    How   *pleasantly*   *the little bird*   *sings*

6

friend - ship and love   our   souls‿ will blend. _____
и бла - го - дат - но   слън - це - то грей. _____
i bla - go - dat - no   slun - tse - to grey. _____
and what a blessing   *the sun*   *shines!*

13

Light - er our bur - den grows   when, with a friend so close,
Рос - ни ли - ва - ди - те,   све - жи по - ля - ни - те,
Ros-sni li - va - di - te,   sve-ji po - lya - ni - te,
Dewy   *the meadows.*   *fresh*   *the grass.*

20

feel-ings and thoughts so   high   meet eye to eye. _____
и - гра - ем ний   и   пе - ем в ра - ни - на. _____
i - gra-em ni   i   pe - em f ra - ni - na. _____
dance   *we*   *and*   *sing*   *at early hour.*

26

Bles-sings a - bun - dant flow   through ev-ery soul, _____
Жи - во - та е кра - сив   и и - зо - би - лен,
Ji - vo - ta e kras - sif   i i - zo - bee - len,
Life   *is*   *beautiful*   *and*   *bounteous,*

32

we feel the Hand Di - vine   mak-ing us whole. _____
че Бог над на - зи е _____ ми - ло - стив. _____
che Bog nad na - zi e _____ mi - los - tif. _____
for   *God*   *over*   *us*   *is*   *merciful.*

23. A Beautiful Day

1st refrain: hands on hips.   *Verse 1:* hands rise alternately.   *2nd refrain:* inside hands hold constantly.
Verse 2 & last refrain: outside and inside hands hold alternately, the outer hands describing and retracing a spacious arc.

Andante (♩. = 58)

End-less_ beau-ty brings the_ spring: heav'n and_ earth with mu-sic_ ring,

liv - ing_ joy   in   ev - ery - thing,   bran - ches,_ blos - soms,_

bub - bling__ springs.   All   a - round   in   daz - zling_ rings,

an - gels_ spread their rain - bow_ wings   o - ver_ ev - ery_

(3rd time) Fine

soul   that_ sings,   o - ver_ ev - ery_ soul   that_ sings.

1. As   we_ wel - come each   new_ day,   from   the_ sun   a
2. Then   God_ whis - pers   in   our_ heart,   "Life   Di - vine   to -

shin - ing_ ray   fills   with_ fire   our heart's de - sire   to
- day   you_ start.   Praise   with_ song   the   life   you're_ giv - en,

see,   to_ hear,   to   live   a - new,   learn - ing_ Love   and
bless   each_ soul   up - on   your_ path,   e - ver_ grate - ful,

D.C.

Wis - dom_ true,   learn - ing_ Love   and   Wis - dom_ true.
e - ver_ glad,   e - ver_ grate - ful,   e - ver_ glad".

24. How Happy We Are

Repeat the entire song. If the extended version is played, join in again when the theme returns.

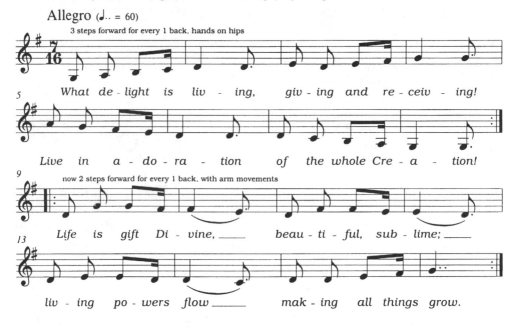

What de - light is liv - ing,   giv - ing and re - ceiv - ing!

Live in   a - do - ra - tion   of   the whole Cre - a - tion!

Life is   gift Di - vine, ____   beau - ti - ful, sub - lime; ____

liv - ing po - wers flow ____   mak - ing all things grow.

25. Step by Step

Step _ by step _ in life we rise, e - ver grow - ing good and wise;

ne - ver hur - ry, ne - ver stop,   till ___ we reach _ the

high - est top.   Fear - less and po - wer-ful, no - thing an ob - sta - cle,

con - scious-ly right - ing ev - ery wrong,   step out stea - di - ly,

help _ out rea - di - ly, blaz - ing a path-way of light in song.

Ris - ing in life __ by slow deg - rees, learn-ing from na - ture's

flowers and _ trees how in due sea - son deep-ly her rea - son

per-fect com-ple - tion sees. Na-ture in win - ter is __ at rest,

like a good mo - ther she knows _ best when to a - wa - ken

plants __ to life, __ when birds _ should build their nest.

E - ver glan-cing for the dan-cing, leap-ing sight _ of a deer;

e - ver lis - tening for the glis-tening sound of run-ning wa-ter clear.

Lost in won - der, breathe in the air. Let the touch of

God, e - very-where bring - ing to blos - som all that is bare,

fill you with life, fill you with love. Gone_ is ev - ery care!

26. Bright and Early

1. Right toe swings across and round behind steady left foot, hands on hips.
2. Four steps forward, with a little impulse from the held inner hands on each step.
3 & 4: four steps forward, hands stretching forward and returning to hips.

Andante maestoso (♩ = 68)

1 & 2. *Rise! New strength is born   with the first   rays of__ dawn.*
3 & 4. Кой   на   ра - ни - на   ста - ва   да и - грай
         Koi   na   ra - ni - na   sta - va   da i - grai
         Whoever   bright and early   gets up   to   dance

Lov - ing ev - ery   liv - ing soul,   sing and work to   serve the Whole!
Glo - ri - fy - ing God's great name   we a - chieve our high - est aim.
по зе - ле - на - та тре - ва   и на бис - тра - та   po - са,
po ze - le - na - ta tre - va   i na bis - tra - ta   ros - sa,
on   the green   grass   and in   the clear   dew.

All who love the light are free,   for__ their_ way they clear - ly__ see.
той ще бъ - де веч - но млад,   здрав_ и__ ху - бав   и __ бо - гат;
toi shte bu - de vetch-no mlad,   zdrav_ i __ hoo-bav   i __ bo - gat;
he will be   always   young.   healthy and beautiful   and   rich;
ще се у - чи най - до - бре,   ня - ма нив - га   да_ ум - ре.
shte se oot-chi nai - do - bre,   nya - ma neev-ga   da_ oom - re.
will   learn   superbly   and will never   die.

27. Breathing and Singing

Moderato, senza misura (♩ = c 72)

(violin)
Ah _____   (3 times)   Ah _____   (3 times)

Ah _____   (3 times)

28. The Blessing

either

*May the peace of God
and the pure joy of God
rise and rest in our hearts
for ever.*

(3 times)

or, stressing the accented syllables

Да пребъде Божият мир и да изгрее Божията радост
Da prebúde Bójiat mír i da izgré Bójiata rádost
May last forever God's   peace and may rise God's   joy

и Божието веселие в нашите сърца.
i Bójieto vessélie f náshte surtsá.
and God's gladness in our   hearts.

II

The Sunbeams

Allegro (♩.. = 60)

arms swing up to left   *clap with right step*   *back*

1. Bright and glo - rious spring-time dawn is break - ing,

forward   *up to right*   *back*   *etc.*

for new life the sleep - ing earth a - wa - king;

with a light and rhyth - mic step we hail the ris - ing day,

(after 3rd clap) hands on hips to return

on the moun-tain mea-dows in ar - ray, with hearts full and gay.

right toe swings over left   *behind*   *over*

2. Sum - mits, lakes and foun - tains flow - ing ring with mu - sic,

behind   *step forward*

sun - shine, on the wa - ters glow - ing, life in - fus - ing,

na - ture ring - ing with our sing - ing. What a glo - rious

spring! What a glo - rious spring! Hea - ven o - pens

wide its por - tals bles - sings down to bring.

3. Draw from na - ture's bound-less wealth life   a - bun - dant,

glow - ing health;   give   your   gifts __ of Love   to   all

bro-thers who are nee - dy, thus you will   a-chieve your high-est goal,

draw from   na - ture's bound - less wealth   life   a - bun - dant,

glow - ing health;   give   your   gifts __ of Love   to   all

bro-thers who are nee-dy, thus you will   a-chieve your high-est goal.

4. *Step with grace, turn your face   to the Source whence all boun-ties flow.*

Send your call   to reach all   souls in need, help-ing them to grow.

Share the   joy   of earth   in   her great new   birth, _____

Adagio, ad libitum (♩ = c 40)

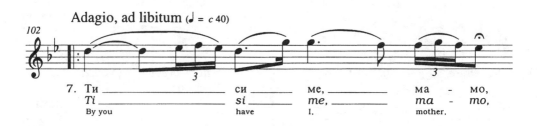

7. Ти _____ си _____ ме, _____ ма - мо,
Ti _____ si _____ me, _____ ma - mo,
By you   have   I.   mother.

чо - век кра - сив   ро - ди - ла, _____
cho - vek kras - sif   ro - di - la, _____
a human being of beauty.   been born.

у - мен да ста - на,
oo - men da sta - na,
wise   to become.

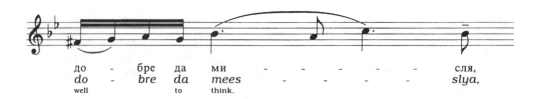

до - бре да ми - - - - - - сля,
do - bre da mees - - - - - - slya,
well   to think.

до - - - бре да лю - - бя:
do - - - bre da lyoo - - bya:
well   to love:

туй жи - во - та е на ра - - - я.
toui ji - vo - ta e na ra - - - ya.
this is the life of paradise.

Allegro (♩.. = 60)

8. Рай, рай, рай, рай, _____ рай, рай, рай, ___ рай, рай, рай, ___
   Rai, rai, rai, rai, _____ *rai, rai, rai,* ___ *rai, rai, rai,* ___
   Paradise.

рай, рай, рай, ___ рай, рай, рай, ___ рай, туй е рай, ___
rai, rai, rai, ___ *rai, rai, rai,* ___ *rai, toui e rai,* ___
this is paradise.

рай, рай, рай, ___ рай, рай, рай, ___ рай, туй е рай, ___ рай.
rai, rai, rai, ___ *rai, rai, rai,* ___ *rai, toui e rai,* ___ *rai.*

Andante (♪ = 184)

r. over l.   open   l. over r.   open   *etc.*

9. Ка - жи ми, ка - жи ми, ка - жи ми слад - ки ду - ми две.
   Ka - ji mi, ka - ji mi, ka - ji mi slat - ki doo - mi dve.
   Tell   me   sweet   words   two.

r. over l.   open   1.   2.

Твой - те ду - ми две, слад - ки ду - ми две. _____ две.
Tvoi - te doo - mi dve, slat - ki doo - mi dve. _____ *dve.*
Your   words   two.   sweet   words   two.

Adagio (♪ = 160)

10. Туй е рай, туй е рай, туй е рай, туй е рай, рай.
    Toui e rai, toui e rai, toui e rai, toui e rai, rai.
    This   is   paradise.

III

The Pentagram

The music is repeated 5 times.

Moderato (♩ = 74)

1-2. *Here we come, beam - ing bright, ro - yal bear - ers of Light!*
3-5. Е - то веч и - дем ний, свет - ло-зар - ни лъ-чи;
      E - to vetch i - dem ni, svet - lo-zar - ni lut-chi;
      Here now come we. beaming rays:

From the heights we des-cend, help to earth we would lend.
цар - ски дар но - сим благ, ра - дост, мир и лю - бов,
tsar - ski dar nos - sim blag, ra - dost, mir i lyoo - bof,
a royal gift we bear. blessed: joy. peace and love.

ossia:

Bro - thers, hear_____ our friend - ly call to - day.
свет - ли - на_____ и жи - ва кра - со - та,
svet - li - na_____ i ji - va kras - so - ta,
light and living beauty.

Fine

We bring_ Love____ and free-dom. With the_ Truth clear your way.
сво - бо - да_____ за всич-ки - те ра - зум - ни ду - ши.
svo - bo - da_____ za fsich-ki - te ra - zoom - ni doo - shi.
freedom for all noetic souls.

17

The position of the Head remains constant: only the couple changes.

Vir - tue, Fair-ness, Wis-dom, Love and Truth: these are the paths Di - vine;
Ний сме слън-че - ви   лъ - чи   на   лю - бов - та, дош - ли в све-та,
Ni sme slun-che - vi   lut - chi na   lyoo-bof - ta, dosh - li f sve-ta,
We are sun - - beams   of   love,   coming   in light,

21

as   the stars they shine,   as   the stars they shine!
зло   да по - бе - дим,   мир   да въ - дво - рим.
zlo   da po - be - dim,   mir   da vud - vo - rim.
evil   that we vanquish.   peace   that we bring.

25   Which couple is now the Head?

Earth   is   re - born to - day,   new   life   be - gins;
Със   бла - гост, свет - ли - на,   неж - на   лю - бов
Sus   bla - gost, svet - li - na,   ne - ja   lyoo - bof
With   kindness.   light   and tender   love

29

heav'n - ly an-thems, an - gel hymns to   earth this new life brings.
нов   жи-вот на   ми - лост-та в све - та   да въ - дво - рим.
nof   ji-vot na   mi - los-ta f sve - ta   da vud-vo - rim.
a new   life   of   compassion   in light   may we establish.

The Head and Left Hand turn to align themselves radially, then remain steadfast.
33   The Feet come into line with the Hands.

Fling   high   the ban - ners white,   let   mu - sic   ring!
Със   бла - гост, свет - ли - на,   неж - на   лю - бов
Sus   bla - gost, svet - li - na,   ne - ja   lyoo - bof
With   kindness.   light   and tender   love

37   The Feet and Right Hand, pivoting on the Left Hand, arrive in line with the Head.

Peace and friend-ship, joy un-end-ing brings the com-ing spring.
нов   жи-вот на   ми - лост-та в све - та   да въ - дво - рим.
nof   ji-vot na   mi - los-ta f sve - ta   da vud-vo - rim.
a new   life   of   compassion   in light   may we establish.

D.C.
ma
maestoso

Peter Deunov.

Peter Deunov

The gentle, kindly touch of Peter Deunov's eyes, and the soulfull, joy-filled swing of his music have steadily reached into my being over the years and warmed my heart with his loving presence. Sometimes it was as if a gentle breeze were wafting me along, and at other times he has made his presence known through others.

On occasion, when I have been teaching PanEuRhythmy or talking about him, people have seen him near, or sensed his presence, vibration, or colors. On one bleak winter morning when I was feeling sad and discouraged, my phone rang and a bright voice said, "How are you? Peter Deunov told me to call you." When I later met this remarkable woman in person, she told me that she had for the previous three days been hearing his voice saying, "Call Ardella! Call Ardella!" and finally she had.

That was the start of a most remarkable year, teaching PanEuRhythmy not only in California and all over the USA, but also in Australia, New Zealand and even in Brazil, as well as taking a group of Americans for the first time to the annual PanEuRhythmy camp in the Rila Mountains of Bulgaria.

Sitting there by the spot where he used to pitch his tent, I was moved to tears as I listened to the sheer beauty and loving soulfulness of his music, being played by musicians who, as children, had lived in the community which had grown up around him.

I remembered how, when still living in England, I had been taken to this region during the era of Communist oppression when nobody dared dance the PanEuRhythmy openly, and we quickly, quietly, and wearily made our way up the mountains, past the Seven Sacred Lakes, only to reach the summit in the fog. Finally, in answer to my desperate prayer, the fog had cleared—just for a few brief seconds, but long enough for me to take the last two photos I had been saving for the view from the top—a memory which would carry me through the next ten years.

Now, ten years later, I could sit here once more, this time openly and in the sunshine. This time, after four years of teaching, I had brought a group from the U.S.A. with me, and we were surrounded by close to one thousand people gathered from all over the world to experience these sacred places where he had taught just over half a century ago and where the PanEuRhythmy had been born.

Maria Mitovska, my friend and mentor, told us, as we climbed to the PanEuRhythmy one morning, how in the early 1920's, when Peter Deunov first brought people to camp here among the Seven Sacred Lakes of Rila, an old man had been meditating by one of the lakes. Suddenly he had become aware of beings of light dancing a most exquisite dance of beauty. Afterwards, when he had told the Master, Peter Deunov had smiled and said, "Yes, you have seen right. And one day I will be teaching you all to take part in that dance." And it was in the ensuing two decades that the PanEuRhythmy was gradually given—a few more dances each summer as the people kept returning to this region.

Yes, the PanEuRhythmy is a lifetime's study—so simple to take part in, and yet needing long-term work to master. It is truly an opportunity to engage with the beings of Light and Love and Joy of the Divine world, and enter into communion with one's own soul and the Soul of the Cosmos.

Peter Deunov was born on 12 July, 1864. His father, Konstantin Deunovsky, was a priest in the Bulgarian Orthodox Church. It is said that as a young man, he made his way to Mount Athos in Northern Greece, just south of Bulgaria, thinking his calling was to become a monk. There in a church he was met by an old priest who told him that his path was a different one. He gave him a sacred book, and talked of the approaching end of the five centuries of Turkish oppression in Bulgaria and the new opportunities for the Church.

Konstantin returned home, married, became a priest, and had three children. As a priest, he was innovative, dedicated, and visionary. He worked tirelessly for the liberation of his people from the Turks, and broke with tradition by reading the Gospel at Mass in Bulgarian instead of in Greek. There is a story that later his youngest son, Peter, once asked him about "the book I gave you in the church at that time."

Peter was of a deeply spiritual nature, and insisted on learning the violin, against the protests of those around him who said this would not help him earn a livelihood. All his life, his violin was his constant companion, and he could often be heard even in the small hours of the night playing gently as a soft prayer wafting heavenwards. He was constantly improvising and composing, and later his followers learned to write down his songs to preserve them for posterity.

When he grew up, he worked for a while as a village schoolmaster near the Black Sea. Then, in 1888, he left for the United States. There he studied for seven years—theology at a Methodist Institute in New York, and medicine in Madison, New England.

The people who knew him there spoke of him with awe. He loved to take them on excursions in the countryside and talk to them of the beauty and secrets of nature and the laws and wonders of the universe. At times he would be found alone deep in meditation, from which he would "awake" as from a deep and beautiful dream.

One man, Grablashev, told of how Peter Deunov once invited him to accompany him into the forest. They came to a beautiful lake and a boat took them across to an island in the middle. There a group was solemnly gathered waiting for him, and the twelve of them entered a large hall and sat around a long table. Grablashev had been told not to ask questions or to record any of the proceedings, so this meeting remains a mystery. Some days later Grablashev attempted to retrace their steps, but was totally unable to find a lake in the area.

On his return to Bulgaria in 1895, Peter Deunov did not return to his school-teaching work, but spent some years in comparative seclusion—writing, studying, and often in the mountains in deep prayer and meditation. He was entering into initiation for his life's work and in 1897 received instructions for his future work to sow the seeds of a new Culture of Love.

After this he began work on his *Testament of the Color Rays of Light*—a book which coordinates the color rays of Light with the seven Spirits of God and the seven stars, with key texts from the Bible for use in healing—physical and spiritual.

In 1897 he issued a *Call to my People* and in 1900 an invitation to the first annual convention. When the only three who turned up asked where all the others were, Peter Deunov replied, "Now you are only three people, but you will become thousands.... The hall is not empty. The chairs are occupied by invisible beings." By the end of his lifetime there were about 40,000 people following his teachings.

I am reminded of how, when the Maharishi Mahesh Yogi first came to London, they hired a large concert hall and issued many invitations. When no one turned up, he insisted nevertheless on giving his full talk, saying that the hall was full of invisible beings and one day would be filled with visible human beings—a prediction which was fulfilled over and over again in his years of popularizing meditation in the West.

I often remember this when I am invited to teach PanEuRhythmy and very few people turn up. As Jesus said, "If you have faith, even as a grain of mustard seed..." If the seed is sown on fertile soil, it matters not how few come, the seed will multiply a hundred-fold.

In the first few years of the twentieth century, Peter Deunov travelled round the country extensively, studying the people carefully. As well as being a musician, violinist, and composer of a very high order, he was skilled in medicine, healing, and phrenology, and accounts of his healings—often miraculous—abound. People gathered around him to learn from his wisdom and be renewed by his love.

In 1905 he settled in a small apartment in Sofia, the capital. People would gather there at 5 AM before going to work, to hear his early morning lectures, often standing in the street even in the snow in winter while he spoke at the window, since there was not room for all indoors. Later, a center was built for him on the hill to the east of Sofia and called "Izgrev" (meaning "Sunrise") since it was here that they first gathered for the sunrise meditation and exercises. Here again he lived very simply in a small room above the meeting hall and library, with just a bed, a table, and a chair. From this room people would often hear sweet strains of music from his violin, even in the very early hours of the morning, long before the time for the lecture at 5 AM. Gradually, people began to buy land and build around, and the community of Izgrev grew.

The annual conventions started in 1900 continued and grew in strength and power. They were now held in the high mountains when the snow melted in July and August, for Peter Deunov maintained that, in order to truly connect with our Soul and Spirit, it is important to rise beyond the astral vibrations of civilization by going at least once a year up into the mountains above the tree-line.

Peter Deunov.

People of all ages would join him, and though the weather was often rigorous, no one was ever ill—even though in the early days they would sleep out under the stars.

The two favorite regions for the mountain camps were near the highest mountain of all, Moussallá (meaning "close to God") and among the Seven Sacred Lakes of Rila—and it was here that the PanEuRhythmy was born. Each summer a few more movements were given, from the early 1920's until finally **The Sunbeams** were added just after the outbreak of World War II. The glorious message of hope and the ultimate triumph of good over evil sounding in the words of **The Pentagram**, given shortly before, must have revived the sinking spirits of many during the darkest period of the century:

> *Here we come, from the Sun,*
> *rays bearing Light.*
> *From the heights we descend;*
> *Help to Earth we would lend.*
> *Brothers, hear our friendly call today:*
> *We bring Love and Freedom, with the Truth*
> *Clear your way....*

Ironically, the entirety of the PanEuRhythmy, together with **The Sunbeams** and **The Pentagram**, were never able to be performed in the mountains during Peter Deunov's lifetime. For that, humanity had to wait the forty-five years after his death that he predicted would pass before the world was ready for his teachings.

It was during these forty-five years that I had the privilege of learning the PanEuRhythmy and connecting with those brave souls who were continuing to practice it and keep it alive until the day when it would at last be able to come out again into the open—in 1989 when the iron hand of the KGB was released. Those visits in secret during the years of harsh oppression and danger are very precious to me, for it was then that I got to know the ones who were close to the Master and who are now no longer with us. Their Light and Joy and Wisdom will ever be in my soul, and I am particularly thankful to Brother Boris Nikolov (generally regarded as the father of the movement) for giving me his blessing to bring PanEuRhythmy to the USA. I am also grateful for the rigorous training I received from Brother Kroum Vagarov with Maria

Mitovska—giving me the confidence of learning the precision of the movements. Kroum and Boris were very close to Peter Deunov for over twenty years, and were key members of the inner circle of his esoteric school. Kroum was married to Yarmila Mentzlova, the student of Isadora Duncan who wrote a book on PanEuRhythmy (in French and now out of print) at Peter Deunov's request.

Peter Deunov himself would usually take part in the PanEuRhythmy, leading from within the circle, while the orchestra played at the center, or sometimes he would watch from the outside. He would encourage people to let the PanEuRhythmy engage their full attention, for in this way the benefits are manifested most fully. The music, singing, movements, and inner meaning can each more than occupy one's full consciousness, so there is never any room for boredom. On the contrary, the more PanEuRhythmy is practiced, the fuller and deeper the experience and the energy gained for the rest of the day.

Peter Deunov always encouraged people to attune to nature and spend as much time as possible out of doors, particularly in the early hours of the day, when the sunlight discharges the greatest spiritual healing and revitalizing energy and quickens the spirit.

The day starts by experiencing the radiance of the dawn before sunrise, for it is at this time that the spiritual energies enter our atmosphere most profoundly. People sit and contemplate the dawn for half an hour or more until sunrise when they rise and raise their right hands to receive the first rays of the sun.[1] They then join in songs of joy and Divine contemplation. From the first day of spring until the fall equinox, this is followed by breakfast and PanEuRhythmy—as much as one has time and inclination for. On Sundays and special occasions, the PanEuRhythmy is danced all the way through, followed by **The Sunbeams** and **The Pentagram**. For those who wish, there are also other exercises done without music— The Seven Sunrise breathing and meditative exercises, and a series of twenty-eight exercises for rejuvenation of each part of the physical and subtle bodies. All these practices are best done out of doors and provide excellent opportunities for re-energizing oneself in communion with nature.

---

1. Care should, of course, always be taken to avoid damage to the eyes from gazing directly at the sun once it has risen.

At this point I would like to share with you excerpts from an account of life in the annual summer camp in the Rila Mountains of Bulgaria, written by Stephen Bonn who came with us last summer.

My Bulgarian Pilgrimage

Going into the Rila Mountain region was like stepping back in time. Riding through the plains approaching the mountains, in an old Russian car, we passed people on the roadside with horse-drawn wagons. At the base of the trail leading to the Seven Lakes, we dropped off our heavy luggage for porters with horses to take up to camp. Later, we saw goatherds with their goats in the mountains. This closeness to the earth was deeply impressive.

Waiting for our guide to come down from the Seven Lakes, we met an interesting couple from France, who spoke English and were waiting to go with us to the same campsite. They are followers of Omraam Mikael Aivanhov. Many people were converging on this base camp. A busload of Russians arrived. We met an older but sturdy Bulgarian woman, who would be carrying all of her provisions on her back.

Our guides arrived, and we started up the trail. During the three hour journey we passed through various landscapes as we increased our elevation. Initially, the trees were tall, and there were areas with numerous raspberries and blueberries. Eventually, at higher elevations, we got to a landscape of shrubs and low trees. At a rest stop, a guide pointed out the Sleeping Giant Mountain in the distance, so named for its resemblance to a sleeping man. Legend has it that Orpheus defeated a giant that is now sleeping as this mountain, and that one should be careful not to "wake the giant."

The Rila Mountains were a site for Orpheus and his mystery school, which makes them anciently sacred. According to Master Beinsa Douno,[1] these are one of three major mountain sites of esoteric initiation in the world, the other two being the Himalayas and the Alps. The Rila Mountains are very ancient and are supposed to be the only mountain range which was never under

---

1. The spiritual name adopted by Master Peter Deunov.

water. High invisible beings are said to live in these mountains, who can bless those who visit here with the proper reverence (and punish those who use the area irreverently, for instance by fishing in the lakes).

We eventually passed the First Lake, and soon afterward, our trail became steep and rocky. After we passed this more challenging portion, we arrived at the first of the campgrounds of the White Brotherhood.[1] Eventually, we arrived at our campsite, and were happily greeted by our Bulgarian hosts.

Life in camp was rugged but wondrous. Our campsite was near the top of a hill, between the Second Lake and the Lake of Purity. Our hosts had done a marvelous job of preparing the campsite with tents, a kitchen area, and a primitive latrine. Water was to be fetched from the sacred spring at the base of the hill between the Second and Third Lakes. This spring has water pouring out of marble "hands" that were carved by disciples of the Master. Various sacred symbols are carved in the surrounding rocks. A large boulder that appears to rest precariously on a small base near the spring is the subject of one of the many stories about the Master. Although he generally preferred not to make a show of his powers, at least once he pointed to this boulder and made it rock back and forth. I believe that after hearing this story, I tried to push the boulder and it wouldn't budge. A flat rock that is painted with a spiral symbol is a place to stand on and make a wish. The Master said that carrying the water up to camp from the spring purifies one's astral body. All this spring magic is great motivation for engaging this hard work.

Before the break of dawn, we would gather at various high places with eastern views, to greet the sunrise. As the dawn peeked over the horizon or through the low-lying clouds, we raised our right hands in communion with it and sang sacred songs from the Master, in Bulgarian. This was followed by prayers and readings, then breakfast—a perfect way to start the day.

In the mornings, we went to various sites to dance the PanEuRhythmy with the Brotherhood. The sites are situated near

1. This centuries-old term for the advanced Souls guiding humanity is often transliterated today as "Fellowship of Light."

various of the lakes. Maria Mitovska, one of our hosts, was my first partner, a graceful dancer, and she had various excellent tips for how to better perform the dance. Various musicians were at the center of the circle, playing violin, guitar, and other instruments. The circle grew larger as we approached the climax of the gathering, which is August 19th, eventually dividing into two, possibly three circles. The inner circles were reserved for those dressed in white. The landscape added much magic to these dances. One day, we danced in a fog and light drizzle, and could barely see the people on the opposite side of the circle. On other days, we were surrounded by majestic peaks in bright clear sky, and truly felt embraced by sacred blessings.

We often went on expeditions in the afternoon, visiting various sites in the surrounding mountains. On one expedition, we were led up a steep cliff, then up a trail, and down to the Sixth Lake. This lake has a crystalline quality about it, which was enhanced by a large ridge of snow that remained near its edge. We were serenaded along the way by one of the PanEuRhythmy violin players, who would stroll ahead of us with seeming ease as we struggled along.

I got severe knee pain on the way down from the above-mentioned expedition. A doctor in the Brotherhood applied a poultice of roasted onions coated with olive oil to my right knee that night, a remedy from the Master. The next day, my knee was much better, and finally, after learning to walk without jarring my heel, the problem more or less was gone.

On the final expedition, we went past the Seventh Lake, and onwards to the highest of the nearby peaks. To explain the lake formations in this region, there are two major groupings of lakes. One is a grouping of seven lakes, with two small lakes to the side. The seven lakes are said to carry the energies of the seven major chakras. The two side lakes are called the Lake of Purity and the Lake of Contemplation, and can be felt to carry the energies corresponding to their names. Near the peak of the high mountain, we were afforded a view of another system of lakes, which were in a landscape of round hills and valleys, colored in a light bluish green. They have a very harmonious quality. Specifically, the Master has spoken of them carrying a feminine magnetic quality about them. Perhaps, in another trip, we will have a chance to absorb this energy by walking through this region. For now, we absorb some of their energy, simply through the beautiful sight of them.

In the evenings, there were concerts held next to the site where the Master used to camp. We heard a beautiful solo performance by a professional tenor, who sang both classical pieces such as Schubert's Ave Maria, and spiritual songs of the Master. Those who know them also sing along with various of these spiritual songs. Concerts were also given sometimes by the PanEuRhythmy musicians, immediately after PanEuRhythmy. Music is a key part of the whole experience here. The "Rila Word Sheet" Ardella provided contained the words to a number of the songs, so we were able to join in on these occasions. Other songs were simple enough to quickly learn and sing along with. I hope to get access to more of this music before my next trip. It can be quite moving.

Like all true and great spiritual Masters, Peter Deunov never made any special claims for himself. He attributed all to the Divine world, and spoke of himself as a servant and mediator of the Divine gifts of healing, teaching, music, and the PanEuRhythmy which came through him. And it is certainly true, in my experience, that PanEuRhythmy is a transmitter of Divine energy, healing, creativity, and joy. It softens and awakens the heart, and makes possible in our lives whatever is the next step in our evolution. Again and again I have experienced people making breakthroughs in their lives with PanEuRhythmy, which had not previously been possible. As one man recently put it, "The next step had been waiting for me for ten years but I had not been able to see it until my mind cleared through the PanEuRhythmy." Another man experienced a major breakthrough in his relationship with his family which twenty-five years of workshops, seminars, and courses had not previously made possible.

I have known some people have significant past-life recalls, while others experience real healing, both physical and emotional, through the PanEuRhythmy. Some develop new abilities and most people's creativity and awareness is heightened. Many people are moved to tears by the deep love and joy they feel and cannot quite understand. For each person, the gift and experience are unique, and improve with wholehearted practice, study, and dedication.

As Peter Dawkins, the great spiritual teacher and founder of the Francis Bacon Research Trust in England wrote,

> The PanEuRhythmy movements are profound in both their effects and their meanings, and learning to become proficient in their practice and to understand them is something that will probably be endless. It is one of the most worthwhile "yogas" for the Western man that we have ever come across... and can relate man in a purely harmonious way with other people and with the whole of nature. It is a great force for brotherhood and peace in the world, and it needs widespread use and study both to do it justice and to make use of what is undoubtedly a great gift to mankind.

Peter Deunov.

Ardella Nathanael.

Ardella Nathanael

Ardella Nathanael is a true global citizen. Raised in West Africa and the Caribbean by British and French parents, Ardella was educated at the Universities of London, Cambridge, Heidelberg, and in Paris, graduating with an Honors degree in French and German, and later with a Social Work Studies Diploma from the London School of Economics.

For nearly a decade, Ardella Nathanael lived and worked in London as a teacher, social worker, and counselor to inner-city families. Fluent in English, French, and German, she taught these languages at all levels and acted as a simultaneous translator for the World Council of Churches and the World Student Christian Federation in Austria, England, France, Sweden and Germany.

Since her youth, Ardella Nathanael has been a student of the world's spiritual traditions and dance. Ardella has studied many forms of dance, including classical ballet, folk dance, sufi dancing and Kathak Kali dance. She coordinated many personal enrichment and meditation classes in London and taught meditation for the British Meditation Society for five years.

Ardella has been a student of PanEuRhythmy since 1983. She braved the Communist regime to learn PanEuRhythmy at secret meetings in Bulgaria started by founder, Peter Deunov. In 1986, she helped introduce PanEuRhythmy in Europe and Great Britain and sponsored the teaching of two Bulgarian teachers.

Ardella Nathanael has been teaching PanEuRhythmy worldwide since 1988. She has introduced thousands of people of all ages to this powerful "Dance of the Soul." She lectures and teaches PanEuRhythmy in the United States, Australia, New Zealand, Great Britain, Europe, Costa Rica, and Brazil.

Information and Products

PanEuRhythmy Practice Cassette

Designed to help the beginner in learning and practicing the PanEuRhythmy, Side A provides, with the music, a continuous running commentary with directions on how to do the movements. Side B again provides the complete music, this time only with cues each time there is a change of movement.

It is an invaluable aid in learning the PanEuRhythmy and best used as a follow-up to a class with a qualified teacher of PanEuRhythmy.

Teaching Videos

These provide a valuable introduction to PanEuRhythmy for those seeking to learn and incorporate it into their lives. Filmed live during a workshop, the videos give an understanding of what PanEuRhythmy is and how it can contribute to our personal lives. They also contain spontaneous questions, discussion, and practice of the group attending the workshop.

Used in conjunction with the PanEuRhythmy Practice Cassette, they enable groups and individuals to get started on learning the PanEuRhythmy in the absence of a true teacher.

Prophet for Our Times by David Lorimer

A profound, knowledgeable, and carefully documented study of the life and teachings of Peter Deunov, the founder of PanEuRhythmy. "His teachings," says David Lorimer, "are essentially a prescription for living in harmony with others, with the earth, and with the Divine, and are relevant to all people whatever their faith or beliefs."

David Lorimer is the founder and director of a charitable foundation based in England for the promotion of the work of Peter Deunov and PanEuRhythmy. He is also the author of several books, the director of the Scientific and Medical Network and the International Association of Near-Death Studies in the United Kingdom. He lectures world-wide on spiritual matters.

For a complete list of all cassettes, videos, pictures, etc., and information on classes in PanEuRhythmy and the other exercises and teachings given by Peter Deunov, contact:

Ardella Nathanael
c/o Tom and Joyce McLellan
2438 Villa Nueva Way
Mountain View CA 94040
USA

Phone: 650/366-2188

For a free catalog of books on Esoteric Philosophy and the Ageless Wisdom, send you name and address to the publisher, or visit us at our website: www.esotericpublishing.com.